Developing Literacy and Creative Writing through Storymaking

Developing Literacy and Creative Writing through Storymaking

Story Strands for 7–12-year-olds

Steve Bowkett

Open University Press

Open University Press
McGraw-Hill Education
McGraw-Hill House
Shoppenhangers Road
Maidenhead
Berkshire
England
SL6 2QL

email: enquiries@openup.co.uk
world wide web: www.openup.co.uk

and Two Penn Plaza, New York, NY 10121–2289, USA

First published 2010

Copyright © Steve Bowkett 2010

All rights reserved. Except for the quotation of short passages for the purposes of criticism and review, no part of this publication may be reproduced, stored in a retrieval system, or transmitted, in any form or by any means, electronic, mechanical, photocopying, recording or otherwise, without the prior written permission of the publisher or a licence from the Copyright Licensing Agency Limited. Details of such licences (for reprographic reproduction) may be obtained from the Copyright Licensing Agency Ltd of Saffron House, 6–10 Kirby Street, London, EC1N 8TS.

A catalogue record of this book is available from the British Library

ISBN-13: 978-0-33-524158-3
ISBN-10: 033524158-1

Library of Congress Cataloging-in-Publication Data
CIP data applied for

Typeset by RefineCatch Limited, Bungay, Suffolk
Printed in the UK by Bell and Bain Ltd, Glasgow.

Fictitious names of companies, products, people, characters and/or data that may be used herein (in case studies or in examples) are not intended to represent any real individual, company, product or event.

Mixed Sources
Product group from well-managed forests and other controlled sources
www.fsc.org Cert no. TT-COC-002769
© 1996 Forest Stewardship Council

FSC

The *McGraw·Hill* Companies

Acknowledgements

My thanks to the artists, also my friends, who prepared the grids for me – Annabel Spenceley for the Anglo Saxon Grid, Tony Hitchman for the Fantasy Grid, Russell Morgan for all other grids. I also want to thank Stella Hender for her evocative drawing of 'Distant Riders' on page 27.

Contents

	Introduction	1

Section 1 Getting Started — 5

1	Picture Masking and Questioning	7
2	Brainstorming and Association Webs	9
3	Summarizing and 'Seed Thoughts'	11
4	Contextualizing and Interpreting	14
5	Sentence Building	17
6	Things Happen for Reasons	21
7	Precise Questioning	24
8	Movie Director	26
9	Zoom In	29
10	Shades of Colour	30

Section 2 Building Narrative — 33

11	Prediction Strips	35
12	Connectives	38
13	Proverbs and Similes	41
14	Back Story	44
15	Story 'Ingredients'	47
16	Cliffhangers	49
17	The Neverending Story	52
18	The Narrative Template	56

Section 3 Enriching the Story — 61

19	Parallel Story	63
20	Story Board Games	65
21	Sequels	68
22	Annotated Margins	71
23	Story Cards	73
24	The Detective Game	76
25	Settings	78
26	Comic Cuts	80
27	Character Creation	82

Section 4 Story Grids — 85

28	Zig Zag Story Game	87
29	Grids and Basic Narrative Elements	89
30	Following the Question Trail	90
31	Making Grids	93
32	Grids and Topic Areas	95
33	Story Strings	97
	Appendix: The Grids	101
	Bibliography	113
	Index	115

Introduction

I have clear memories of my junior school teacher, Mr Evans, telling the class, 'I've got a real treat for you today – you're going to write me a story!' and of the groan that went up from the children. Then Mr Evans smiled and said, 'But don't worry, I'll help you.' And he wrote the title on the board.

It was at that point I suffered (again) from what has been called the fear of the blank page … All of this white space I'd have to fill with words and sentences that not only must be grammatically accurate, but were also expected to be correctly spelled and punctuated *and* neat. Even now, all these years later when I have written millions of words, I can still feel echoes of that dread and wonder how I ever came to write any stories at school at all. Because there's no doubt that creative writing can be a daunting and difficult task, for many reasons. The two most fundamental ones I feel, on which all the others rest, are

1   How can I have ideas?
2   How can I organize those ideas?

The central problem is that creativity (in any field) amounts to making new connections. This often comes about by being able to look at things in a variety of ways; to take a 'multiple perspective' on the problem. When a new connection is made, the result is an original idea. Basically this is to say that it originated in the mind of the thinker. The idea may be commonplace as far as everybody else is concerned, but to the 'originator' it is new and fresh and comes with the pleasant feelings that are part and parcel of such a 'Eureka!' moment. It should go without saying that the more practice a child has at being original at this individual level, the greater the chances of them one day having truly original thoughts that are new to everyone.

However any piece of writing is made up not just of one idea but of many put together in a coherent way and according to an overall plan. Such a plan will ideally conform to the conventions of the genre (using the word here to include also the various kinds of non-fiction) and the conventions of form, which include the style of the writing itself. In other words, a story for instance will have a certain recognizable form and structure (hero, villain, problem, setting; be arranged into scenes and paragraphs, etc.) that will distinguish it from a poem or a set of instructions or a newspaper article. (Although having said that, these categories can be blurred to suit a writer's purpose, when they are deliberately being *un*conventional.)

The resource of the imagination can be used very flexibly. First although it is difficult to force ideas by 'trying hard to think', techniques like the ones in this book help to provide structure and focus for thinking such that sound and usable ideas often then pop into the mind by themselves. So what we are trying to develop in children when we ask them to write a story is a network of skills, which are best cultivated when young writers feel engaged, capable and excited. When this happens the abilities that are simplistically lumped together under the heading of 'literacy' will emerge in an organic and more enjoyable way. 'Literacy' incidentally is not very helpfully defined as the ability to read and write. What I have been talking about, and what I hope all of us want to achieve, is going beyond this to help children to take ownership of language; allowing them to play with it, test it, challenge it and ultimately to forge out of it something new and individual and vital.

Practical tips for using the book

The techniques in this book, and in other books I have written, aim to be practical and applicable across a wide age and ability range. The 'story strand' activities are sequenced from the simplest towards the more complex. However you may choose to use them individually or in any order to create your own programmes to suit your particular needs.

The activities in the book are accompanied by extra resources you can access from the Open UP website. As well as additional activities and a Glossary, you'll be able to download all the grids found at the back of the book, plus a fully worked example of how images can be used to create a dice game. 'The Search for the Kay-to-Bah Diamond' demonstrates how making such a game has value for children in terms of planning, instructional writing, using 'the vocabulary of the genre' (see page 10) and numeracy.

All of the activities incorporate flexibility within a structure. That is to say they are not so vague as to leave children floundering, but not so prescriptive that children have no room to think for themselves. Beyond that I would offer the following advice:

- Avoid 'overwhelm'. Don't ask the children to do too many things at once. One valuable example would be to encourage children not to worry about neatness and spelling as they're having ideas and beginning to organize them. Attending to technical accuracy can come later.

- Make no judgements about the quality of the children's ideas early on in the writing process. That is, don't compare the quality of one child's work against another's at this point. Having said that, offer sincere praise wherever possible – and *be specific*. Say exactly what it is about the writing that you like.

- Model the attitude. When you want the children to write creatively, have a go yourself. Feel free to talk about your experience with the class. If you're having difficulty say so, and ask the children how the problem may be solved. When you're pleased with something you've written, show your pleasure (and say why you are pleased).

- Transfer the skills (embedded in the creative attitude). All learning requires children to engage with language and to doubt, challenge and question ideas. Thus what they learn about having and organizing ideas in the context of creative writing will be useful across the curriculum.

- When you see a blank page encourage the children to think 'Oh wow, how can I possibly fit all of my ideas into that small space?'

Using images to stimulate creative writing

This is not a new idea of course: most of us in the classroom will have asked children to base a piece of writing – not only a story – on a picture. At worst it amounts to an instruction to 'Look at this picture then write a story about it', which is not teaching creative writing in any way that I recognize.

However as the old saying goes, a picture is worth a thousand words. Well, whether that value judgement is true or not, a picture can *evoke* a thousand words. And a number of pictures used together can lead to much more than that.

My aim in this book is to explain how to use pictures and simple images to help children generate and organize ideas in a systematic way. The activities are sequenced but you can use them in any order. Having said that, I suggest you look at them in sequence first to get the 'big picture', as it were. That overview will inform you as you recommend combinations of story strand activities to particular children.

One more thing – though by now perhaps I'm overindulging in reminiscence – something else I remember from primary school is that Mr Evans didn't like us to put drawings in with our stories. He thought that by Year 5 we'd outgrown that. I'll be encouraging children to 'draw out' their ideas as well as write about them. In this way they will be enriching the picture resources already provided and developing (in a visual world) their 'visual literacy' also.

SECTION 1
Getting Started

CHAPTER 1

Picture Masking and Questioning

Activity

Select a suitable picture (one that will stimulate discussion) and mask it so that only a part of it is visible. Encourage children to ask questions as they explore possible scenarios. Using the 'Big Six' question words gives children a platform for their enquiry – what, where, when, who, why, how. Note that at this stage we're not looking for answers to the questions. This takes away any pressure to try and think of a 'right' or even a reasonable answer. It also communicates the vitally important message that it's fine not to know at this stage. This translates into the educationally valid notion that children's ability to 'learn how to learn' is supported when they can feel comfortable in an environment of ambiguity and uncertainty.

Learning benefits

As well as the points above, this activity

- encourages speculation and the exploration of possibilities
- introduces/reinforces the notion of 'reasonableness' when having ideas
- promotes discussion in the context of collaborative enquiry.

Taking it further

- Focus on one of the Big Six question words at a time. For instance say 'Let's think of as many *what* questions as we can.' Record ideas as they appear.
- **Mind Mapping**. If you systematically focus on one question word at a time, consolidate the information as a mind map. Put the masked picture in the middle of the visual field (large sheet of paper, IWB, etc.). Put the Big Six question words around the central image and 'cluster' children's

ideas around the appropriate key word. Note that colour coding the key words and children's ideas makes the mind map easier to access when a lot of information has accumulated.

- **The Maybe Hand**. Ask the class to pretend that the masked picture is in the middle of an open hand. Take one of the questions already generated, such as 'Where is he going?' Now ask the children to think of five possible answers. Use the word 'maybe' each time. So, maybe he's going home/maybe he's going to rob a bank, etc. Using this technique
    - gives children a visual and tactile analogue to the mental structure of speculation. The focus of the thinking is in the palm of the hand and five possible explanations radiate away from it.
    - encourages children to generate at least five ideas each time they use the technique. Note that this technique can be used across the curriculum whenever you want children to speculate.

- **If–Then games**. Once you have a stock of possible explanations, try out the following techniques.
    - **The simple If–Then game** selects a possibility and asks children to come up with one consequence arising from it. So, if he was going to rob a bank – then he'd have to be careful the police didn't find him. Children can make up as many if–thens as they like, but in each case the pattern remains one possibility linked to one consequence.
    - **If–Then–So maybe . . .** This more complex pattern takes speculation further. *If* he was going to rob a bank – *then* he'd have to be careful the police didn't find him – *so maybe* he'd disguise himself and travel to a different part of the country. Here we have a speculation built on a speculation. Create an even greater challenge by asking children to think of five so maybes each time!

- **What's reasonable?** Using the basic Maybe Hand game, when children have five possible answers to a question, ask them to put them in order of reasonableness or likelihood or 'ordinariness'. So 'maybe he's going home' is a more ordinary and perhaps likely explanation than 'maybe he's going to rob a bank'. Make it clear to the children that they won't have to use the most ordinary or 'reasonable' ideas in their stories! Ideas can be wild and wacky, but in all good stories *things happen for reasons the reader can accept*. This activity also helps children to stop their imaginations running away with themselves.

- **Unmasking**. Once you have a range of questions based on the masked picture, reveal more of the picture. This will serve to generate further speculation. It also creates the opportunity for children to *modify their earlier ideas in light of further evidence*. This emerging skill can usefully be applied in science.

CHAPTER 2

Brainstorming and Association Webs

Activity

Children are given or choose a simple picture and are invited to write down any words they associate with the image. (See Figure 2.1).

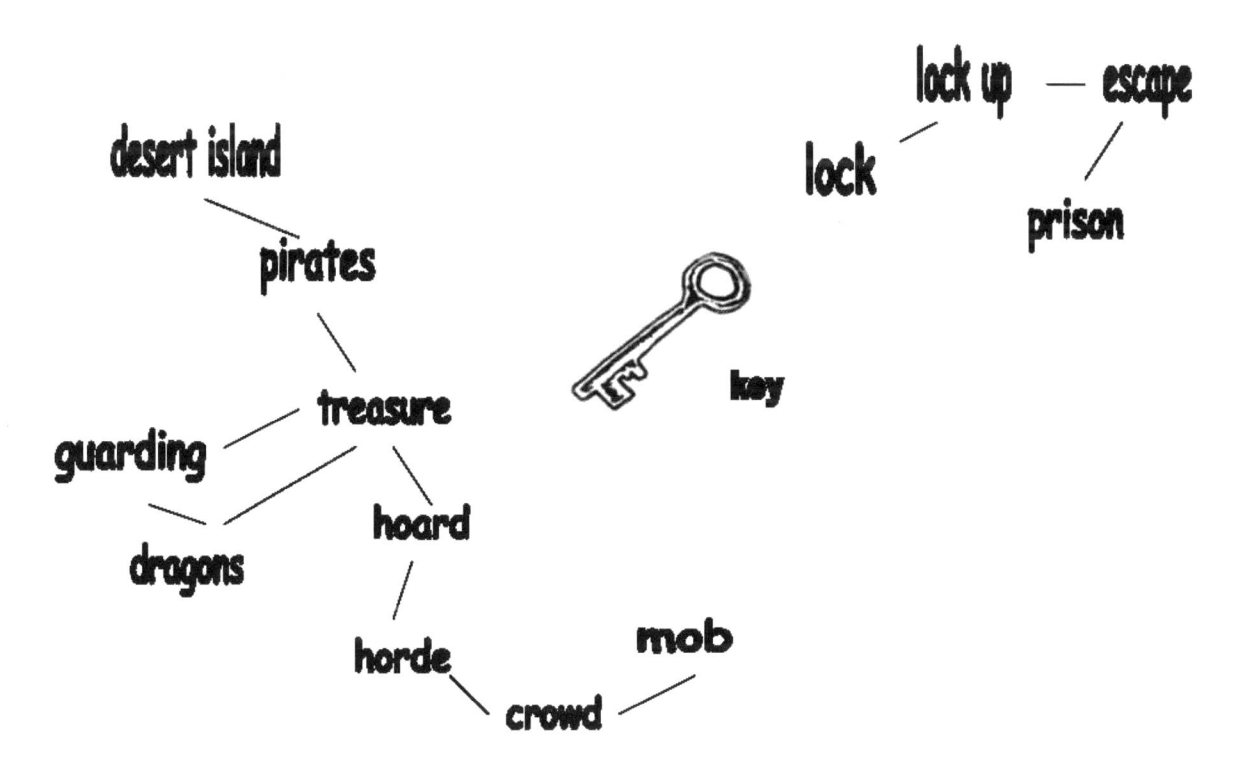

desert island
pirates
guarding
treasure
dragons
hoard
horde
crowd
mob

lock up — escape
lock
prison
key

Figure 2.1

👍 Learning benefits

- Children accumulate vocabulary they can use later in their writing.
- The activity places an emphasis on the selection of appropriate/effective words rather than the first ones that spring to mind.
- It creates the opportunity to explore homophones (hoard/horde), synonyms (crowd/mob) and other features of the language.
- Using genre-specific images, children learn the 'vocabulary of the genre' more thoroughly. As new key words and other vocabulary are introduced by the adult in the classroom and other children, young writers can more easily link them with the words they already know and incorporate these new ideas into their growing word web.

Taking it further

Extend the activity by introducing further pictures to build into the expanding word web. Put the images on the edge of the page. When a child sees an opportunity to incorporate an image they place it near the associated word. The group then 'grows' the web around both images. So, for instance, placing a picture of a bottle near 'desert island' may lead to additions such as message-in-a-bottle/thirst/water/litter/rum/ship-in-a-bottle and so on. Encourage children to make further creative links by naming both images in a sentence – 'The bottle was the key because …?'/'How did the key get into the bottle?', etc.

! Subject link

Encourage children to incorporate ideas from topics they have previously covered into their word webs. Using the example above, weather and climate words, pirate-related words (cutlass, doubloons, etc.) might be added. This offers a useful opportunity for revision.

CHAPTER 3

Summarizing and 'Seed Thoughts'

Activity

Children pick any two pictures/words from a selection. If they were to use them in a story, what would the story be about? Encourage the children to summarize their idea in a sentence or two. Look out for – and do not allow – 'and thens'. These indicate that the child is making up the story 'off the top of the head', snatching at the first thought that comes to mind without reflecting, reasoning or making any judgements about appropriateness, logical consistency, etc.

So for example, choosing these two items from the selection below (see Figure 3.1)

Figure 3.1

Might produce ideas such as:

- A man reads about buried treasure in an old book, then hires a boat to try and find it.
- A young boy reads about sailing around the world and decides he'll do it too!
- Our hero is researching the mysterious disappearance of some people from a boat when they went rowing on the lake.

Learning benefits

- Children gain experience in taking multiple perspectives on ideas. This is a key element of creativity, together with finding links between smaller ideas to create information.
- Children learn to have greater control of their imagination because of the constraints of the task.
- Young writers are encouraged to make a few well chosen words do a lot of work, the key aspect of succinctness.
- There is also the more implicit benefit of helping children to realize that even a simple resource (a small number of words and images) can have great potential.

12 GETTING STARTED

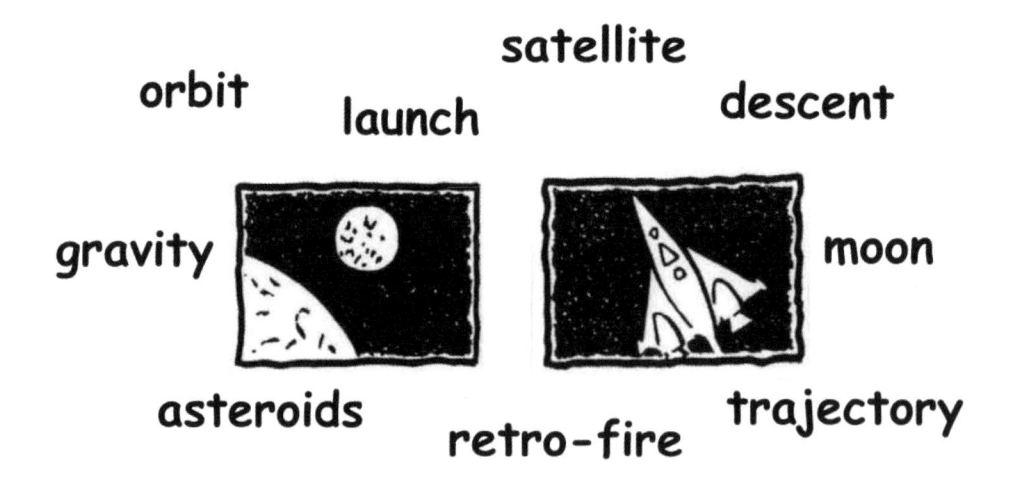

orbit launch satellite descent
gravity moon
asteroids retro-fire trajectory

Figure 3.2

Taking it further

- Reversing the sequence of images will often produce further ideas . . .
    - A group of girls picnicking at the lake find a magic spellbook in an empty, drifting boat.
    - A man makes a dangerous sea crossing to buy a rare book he wants to sell for a great profit. But other people want it too.
    - A wizard creates a book telling you how to build a boat that can sail through time.

- Note that in the same way that you can extend the creative and intellectual challenge to children by increasing the number of images for them to talk about, encourage young writers to build sentences by progressively using more words from the selection:
    - The rocket was launched.
    - The rocket was launched into orbit.
    - The rocket was launched on a trajectory to the moon.

- Explore differences of meaning between superficially similar words. What's the difference between a satellite and a moon or an orbit and a trajectory?

- Although children are working on stories, they are still using the vocabulary of a 'real' subject, and in appropriate contexts. Take advantage of this by, for instance, running a science topic on space concurrently with their storymaking.

Practical tips

- Using genre-specific images will help to keep children focused and encourage them to use the 'vocabulary of the genre' more appropriately. Guide young writers further by having key words available as images are selected. (See Figure 3.2).
- Asking children to confine their ideas to just two images is not limiting their thinking but rather allowing them to control their imaginations. Besides, the immediate aim of the activity is to have children summarize an idea, not elaborate upon it on the spur

of the moment. Another benefit of such a summary is that it acts as a 'seed thought'. Once that first creative link has been made, the story is usually assimilated further, often at a subconscious level, so that more ideas and narrative developments pop into mind without children having to try and force them or struggle to move the story on.

- When young writers are familiar with this game and create two-image summaries with ease, suggest that they might try a three-image summary, then four, etc. Often children will raise the creative challenge for themselves, so that it isn't unusual for a child to say 'Well I can do it with five!' To which his friend replies, 'Well I can do it with six!'

- Allow such positive competition by all means, but 'keep the activity tight' by insisting that summaries are brief and to the point.

Taking it even further

- Develop the power and flexibility of the children's thinking by cutting out a number of images and placing them face down on the table. Turn up two and create a summary. Then turn up a third image – how would that add to the story? Now turn up a fourth image – how and where would it fit into the developing narrative? Continue until either the story seems 'rounded' and complete (in which case further images would complicate matters), or all the images have been used. In this latter case, if the story is still not finished, ask the children to decide which images could be added to do that job.

- Do the same as above, but this time have the images face up. Choose two for a summary, then work with the children to *discuss* which other images can now be added, and in which order, to build the narrative.

CHAPTER 4

Contextualizing and Interpreting

Activity

Narratives are linked sequences of ideas that explore a context or 'field' of thinking. Earlier games such as making association webs encourage children to make links in this way, although the connections are often quite 'loose' and free ranging. Formalizing the activity by preparing strips of images such as the one below (see Figure 4.1) guides children towards the 'linear linking' that mirrors the way in which sentences and stories are constructed. Encourage children to build the context of a story by showing them a sequence of images with gaps, as in Figure 4.1.

Figure 4.1

- Ask children to select other images to fill the gaps, then suggest how the whole sequence could form a simple storyline.
- **Story on-the-hoof**. Ask each group or child to create a strip of images: they don't need to have a storyline worked out. Pair up the groups so that each larger group can put their sequences together to create a longer 'story strip'. Working collaboratively the children discuss and decide on a more extended storyline. You can go at least one stage further by joining up the paired groups to form a smaller number of 'super groups', each of which now has a four-sequence story strip to talk about. Alternatively just get paired groups to swap story strips so each has a new two-sequence strip to work on.
- **Story crossword**. Using one or more of the grids you'll find at pages 102–12 (or on the website), have children create a crossword-like arrangement of images as in the image in Figure 4.2. Ask each group to decide on a first image and a final image. The task then is to use all of the images in between to create a storyline. Extend the game by using the 'missing' images: children take one or more of these and attach them to the start and/or the end of the storyline, thus extending the story and encouraging the creation of new and different beginnings and ends.

CONTEXTUALIZING AND INTERPRETING 15

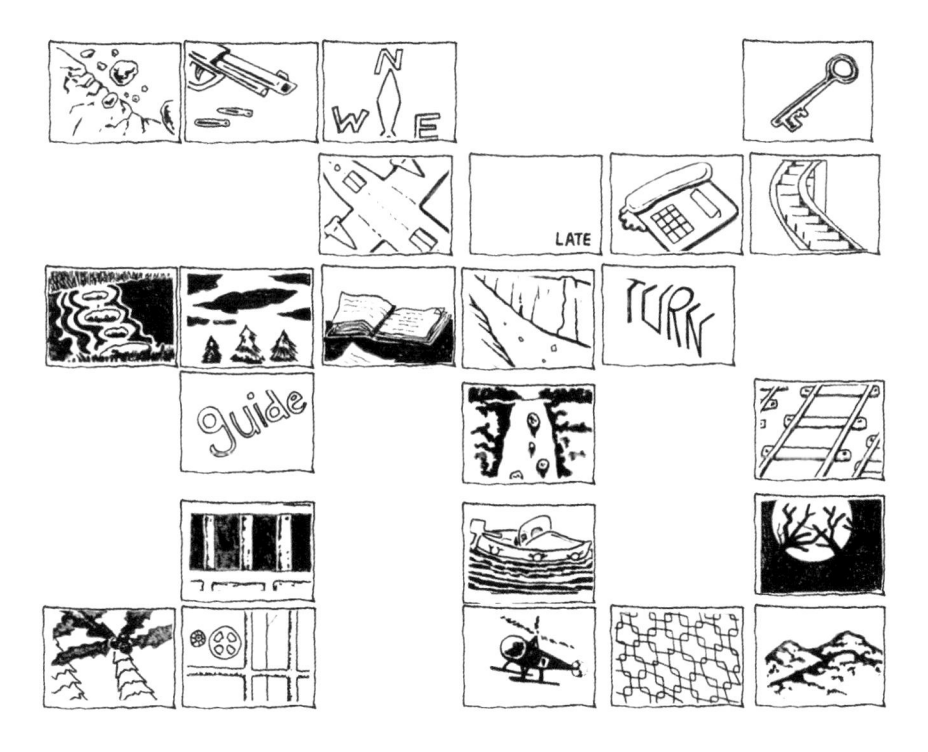

Figure 4.2

👍 Learning benefits

- The activity develops the skill of seeing the bigger picture.
- It encourages the children to build rationales to support their interpretations (by the use of logical connectives for instance – then, finally, furthermore, also, however, because, etc.

Taking it further

- The pattern above could be intended as just the start of a longer story, in which case the 'story strip' would end up being much longer than this (more on that later). Or the picture sequence might indicate key scenes or events across the whole span of the narrative. Once the sequence has been completed by filling the gaps, ask children to summarize the story in a few sentences.

- Another way of extending the game is to show a sequence with gaps, or with all boxes filled, and imagine that the events it suggests happen in the *middle* of the story, as in Figure 4.3. In which case, how might the story start, develop, reach a climax and resolve? Using this variation of the story strip idea helps to make children's thinking more flexible. In my experience children often feel they have to 'get the beginning right' before they can concentrate on the rest of the story. They are correctly taught that stories should have strong openings to involve the reader. They also learn the beginning–middle–end structure at an early age. But when creating a context for the story that is to be written, they may naturally have ideas about any part of the narrative at any time. Suggesting to them that it's OK to think about the middle (or any part of the story) first is acceptable, and indeed to be encouraged.

    So, for example

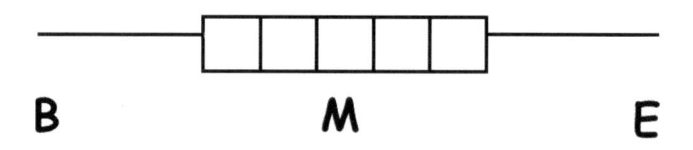

Figure 4.3

- Invite children to play with this idea by giving them large sheets of paper. Draw a horizontal line across the sheet. Then take a story strip and place it somewhere along the line. What could the rest of the story (before and after the strip) be about? Even if the children don't know yet, let them place other images and/or picture sequences elsewhere along the line experimentally and brainstorm a number of possible narratives.

Practical tip

Try following this activity with the Detective Game on pages 76–7 to further develop the children's skills.

Subject link

Make the skill of interpreting explicit in science lessons, for example, and in textual analysis (at whatever level of difficulty) where the key message is 'I think a) because b)'.

CHAPTER 5

Sentence Building

Activity

Strips of images can be used to help children build increasingly complex sentences, paragraphs and scenes. Ask children to write sentences in the blank boxes that incorporate the images on either side (see Figure 5.1).

| | The boy found a book in an old house. | | The house stood beside the road not far from the hills. | |

Figure 5.1

Learning benefits

- Demonstrates a conceptual bridge between simple and complex sentences
- Shows children a way of breaking down the large and complex task of building a narrative into simpler and more manageable stages.
- Creates the opportunity to select words carefully.

Taking it further

- Practise the use of dialogue by imagining two characters having a conversation that incorporates the images along the strip, as in Figure 5.2.

18 GETTING STARTED

> "The map in this book is spot on," said Ben. "Look, there's the old house up ahead."
>
> "Seems a bit spooky to me." Sarah looked worried. "Do you think we should risk going any closer?"
>
> However, the children went inside and spent an hour exploring…
>
> But they failed to find what they were searching for.
>
> "Well that was pretty much a waste of time!" Ben looked annoyed.
>
> Sarah nodded towards the nearby hills.
>
> "Don't give up yet. The arrow on the map points that way. Come on, let's keep going."

Figure 5.2

- Although stories like this tend to be 'made up as they go along', your earlier choice of images will help to prevent children's imaginations from wandering randomly. Also, as children become familiar with this activity they are likely to create more coherent and focused narratives. Encourage this by suggesting they look along the whole strip and think about how the plot might unfold. Ask for several possible storylines. This primes young writers to actively construct stories that have more of a logical consistency, rather than being satisfied with the first ideas that spring to mind.

- Picture strips like these also serve as a 'bridge' between simple and more complex sentences. Begin with a simple sentence, perhaps one related to pictures the children have already been using. See Figs. 5.3 to 5.6 below.

> The boy found a book in an old house.
>
> The house stood beside the road not far from the hills.

Figure 5.3

| The | boy | found | a | book | in an | old | | house | |

Figure 5.4

- Ask for suitable words to fill the gaps ….

| The | *young* | boy | *recently* | found | a | *battered* | book | in an | old | *lonely* | house | *by the roadside* |

Figure 5.5

- Play a game called 'stacking alternatives'. Instead of just one word to fill a gap, ask for a number of suggestions, including phrases ….

	dark haired		*to his great delight*	*	*magical*	*		*derelict*	*spooky*	*	*five miles out of town*
	curious		*unexpectedly*	*	*rare*	*	*in a*		*unvisited*	*	*not far from the highway*
	nosy		*suddenly*	*	*valuable*	*		*ancient*	*desolate*	*	*close to the foothills*
The	*young*	boy	*recently*	found	a	*battered*	book	in an	old	*lonely*	house	*by the roadside*

Figure 5.6

- A variation of the activity calls for the preparation of cards on which are written the names of the parts of speech. So you would have a number of cards with 'noun', 'adjective', 'verb', 'adverb', etc. Also prepare cards with titles such as 'synonym', 'replace with a phrase', 'change tense', etc. If the children are well versed in grammar you could even include more demanding cards such as 'subordinate noun clause', 'verb phrase', 'convert to conditional future tense' and so on (although this level of challenge brings me out in a cold sweat!)

    - Divide the class into paired groups, with perhaps four children per group. Make enough sets of cards for one per group.
    - Start each group off with a simple sentence between them – The boy found a book – and flip a coin to decide which group starts. The starter group turns up a card that the opposing group must respond to. So if the card says 'adjective' the other group must add an adjective to the sentence … 'The boy found an ancient book'. Now it's their turn. Their card might say 'change tense' and so … 'The boy will find an ancient book'.
    - The game continues until a group either runs out of cards or the sentence becomes so unwieldy that its sense is lost. The aim as far as you are concerned is not to produce a winner but to help all of the children to acquire the habit of constructing more complex and yet balanced sentences that have a certain elegance and 'flow'.

Practical tips

Note that in certain places (*) synonyms for words used in the original sentence can be asked for – discovered/came across/stumbled upon … volume/tome/publication … mansion/building/dwelling. This creates an opportunity for using a thesaurus and discussing shades of meaning and the appropriate use of words.

CHAPTER 6

Things Happen for Reasons

I like to tell children about the time I was reading a Fantasy novel and came to a part where 'the dragon breathed purple smoke'. That created a vivid image in my mind, though I was also interested to know *why* the smoke was purple – but the author never explained it and that disappointed me. On one occasion when I made the point that the idea would have been stronger with a reason behind it, one child said, 'If I'd written it, dragons would have breathed smoke of different colours depending on the mood they were in.' Now that *is* a good idea!

Part of thinking through a story is working out the reasons why things happen as they do. This helps to make the tale more believable and gives it a logical consistency. In other words, the story 'hangs together' so that events, descriptive details and so on are acceptable within the context of the narrative. This principle holds true even for Fantasy stories, Horror tales and stories containing lots of wacky off-the-wall humour, where things can so easily happen *just* because they're scary or gory or hilarious. Allowing children 'to get away with it' promotes lazy thinking in my opinion and conveys the message that it's OK to snatch at the first idea that comes to mind. This in turn leads to what I call 'and then' thinking where young writers make up stories as they go along, creating simple chains of events that are sequential but not cohesive. This is acceptable if it's understood the result is a first draft that will be improved later. However the trouble is that if lots of things happen without an underlying reason, the child faces an uphill struggle to create logical consistency within a story that *as a whole* doesn't really work. Trying to fix that can easily take the fun out of writing.

When teaching children about this it's important for them to understand that you aren't being critical of their work. To ask 'why does the dragon breathe purple smoke?' is an opportunity for the writer to think further and come up with a rationale that they can incorporate into the story.

One way of helping is to use the 'Maybe Hand' technique (see page 8) and turn it into a group game. 'Let's think of five possible reasons why the dragon's smoke was purple ... So maybe because ... Or maybe because ..., etc'.

This is also an opportunity to introduce things-happening-for-a-good-reason as a *criterion of quality* within narrative. Try the following game as a way of helping children to generate ideas and build in underlying rationales.

Activity

- Select five images from one of the grids and cut them out.
- Use a star template like the one below and arrange the images at the points, as in Figure 6.1.

Figure 6.1

- Put one or more of the Big Six question words (see page 7) in the centre of the star and brainstorm some questions that link two or more of the images. So –
    - Why did the man fire his gun at the telephone?
    - Why was the key buried under the rocks?
    - How did the man use the map to find the key?
    - What has the key got to do with the telephone?
    - What is the link between the map and the avalanche?

- Now turn the questions into statements and append the word 'because'. The man fired his gun at the telephone because … The key was buried under the rocks because … And so on.
- Now for each statement brainstorm possible answers. Remember that in brainstorming all ideas go into the pot without being judged. So even 'The man fired the gun at the telephone because he hated telephones' is acceptable.
- When you have a stock of ideas plus rationales, look at them one at a time and discuss how strong/believable each one is. Simply talking it through can lead to weak reasons morphing into stronger ones or being discarded, while the more robust reasons are retained.

Practical tip

Weak reasons can often be improved by finding out more with the 'because game'. This attempts to create a chain of reasoned links. So with a rationale such as 'The man fired the gun at the telephone because he hated telephones' you would say 'He hated telephones because …?' Out of the ideas that come forward, take what you think is the strongest and if necessary apply the because-tool again. 'He hated telephones because they frightened him as a child.' 'They frightened him as a child because …?' 'Because when his Mum's ex-husband phoned she always got upset …'

You'll see that what's emerging here is not only a more robust reason for the character shooting at the telephone, but we're learning something about that character's background as well.

Learning benefits

- Children come to understand the importance of logical consistency.
- Critical and reflective thinking skills are developed.
- Young writers come to see more clearly that problems in 'making a story work' can usually be fixed.

CHAPTER 7

Precise Questioning

Activity

- Select the visual resource you want to work with. This might be a single picture, a strip of images, ideas generated by the 'because game' (see page 23) or similar.
- Introduce the class to the kinds of words and phrases that elicit more information from the idea; exactly, precisely, in more detail, tell me more, and also, etc.
- Remind children of the Big Six question words (although not all of them will apply here) – what, where, when, who, why, how.
- Now begin to frame questions using these key words and the 'precision questioning' terms. Here are some examples using the short story strip you met earlier (see Figure 7.1).

Figure 7.1

- What did the book look like in more detail?
- How exactly did the pages sound as the boy flipped through them?
- Tell me more about the room where the boy found the book.
- What else could the boy see from the road apart from the house?
- What precisely was the weather like?

👍 Learning benefits

- Develops the skill of internalizing the attention. This is called metacognition (see Glossary.
- Strengthens the skill of multi-sensory thinking.
- Gives children practice in asking precise questions.

💡 Practical tip

These kinds of questions are also useful as a critical thinking tool when children are confronted by generalizations or engaged in constructive argument and debate. Notice how powerful they are if applied to the following:

- Of course everybody knows that children are lazier now than they were when I was young.
- Technology got the world into this mess and so technology will get us out of it.
- The English are more reserved than Americans but less outgoing than the Italians.

For more information see for example my *Countdown to Non-Fiction Writing* (Bowkett 2009).

CHAPTER 8

Movie Director

Activity

- Select a suitable picture – we'll use the one in Figure 8.1 as our example.
- Ask the children to imagine that the picture is from a scene in a movie they are making and that they are directing and working the camera. As appropriate, introduce the class to the language of film making – slow close up, pan left/right, zoom in, and so on.
- Explain that you will be giving them a few instructions to help them get used to working the camera, but after that it's up to them. Your instructions should be designed to help children a) think in a multisensory way and b) draw more details out of their imagination. So questions might include:
    - Do a slow zoom-in on the riders. As you do their faces become clearer. What do you notice? How would you describe the face of the rider in front?
    - Turn up the sound recording equipment so that you can hear the sound of the horses moving across the ground. Describe what you hear? What other sounds do you notice in your headphones?
    - Pan the camera around slowly to the right. Do a slow full circle. What do you notice about the landscape?

Learning benefits

- Gives practice in internalizing the attention.
- Develops metacognition – the ability to notice, reflect on and manipulate one's own thoughts. This in turn allows children to strengthen further aspects of their imagination, so that a child who is a highly visual thinker, for instance, can practise the skill of listening to mental sounds, exploring imagined textures and so on.
- Children's concentration spans are increased.

MOVIE DIRECTOR 27

Figure 8.1

Practical tip

Any picture you use for this work can later be placed into a 'film strip' featuring blank boxes either side, as in Figure 8.2. Children then write brief notes on what might appear in the boxes if this really were a movie.

28 GETTING STARTED

Filmstrip Technique:

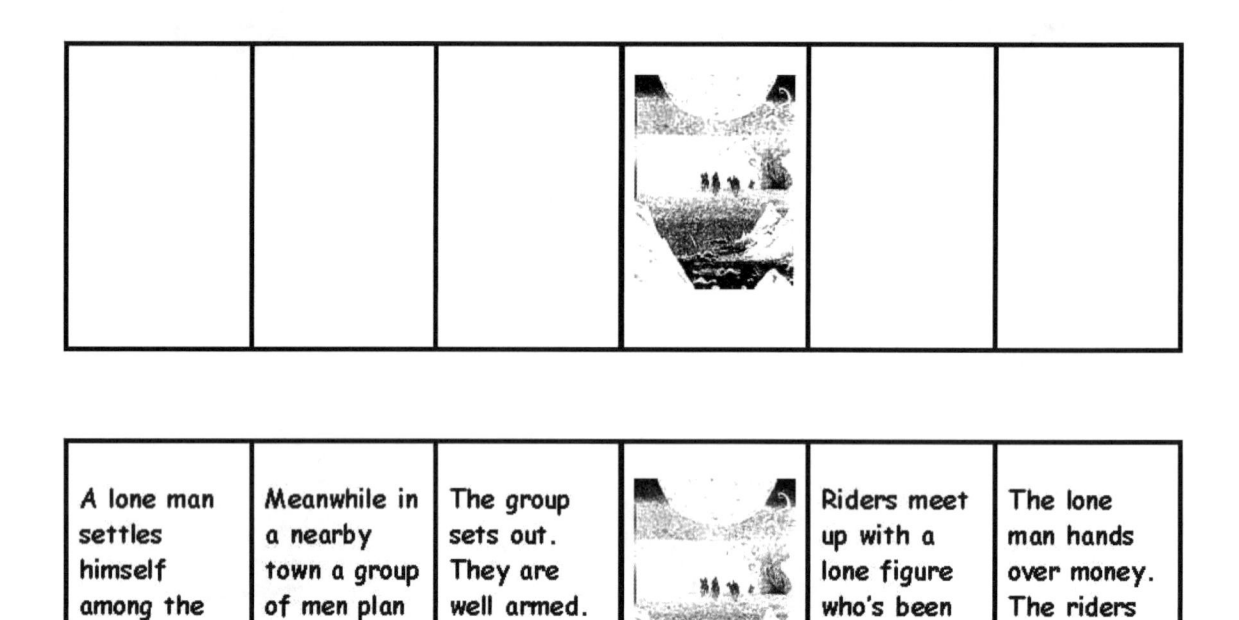

| A lone man settles himself among the rocks to wait. | Meanwhile in a nearby town a group of men plan an ambush. | The group sets out. They are well armed. | | Riders meet up with a lone figure who's been hiding. | The lone man hands over money. The riders give him a map. |

Figure 8.2

CHAPTER 9

Zoom In

Activity

Building on the visualization work of Movie Director (Chapter 8), ask children to imagine that in their mind's eye they have a powerful magnifying glass, microscope or telescope (whichever is most appropriate). Whatever they look at through the lens will be seen in more detail.

So taking an image such as the distant hills (Figure 9.1), imagine looking through a telescope and slowly zooming in …

Figure 9.1

- 'I see small bushes growing on the slopes. They're blowing gently in the wind.'
- 'Now I can see the leaves on the bushes, a kind of pale yellowish green, really dry.'
- 'The ground is like crumbly dirt, a bit chalky. There are lots of small stones.'
- 'The wind is blowing dust about, around the bushes and into the air in little puffs …'

Allowing children actually to look through magnifying glasses and telescopes to give them a real zooming-in experience can enhance the activity.

Learning benefits

Visualizing in this way

- improves concentration
- boosts metacognitive ability
- 'refines the senses' by developing the skill of noticing fine detail, similarities and differences.

CHAPTER 10

Shades of Colour

The skills that children develop by concentrating inwardly in this way can be further strengthened by having them notice details 'on the outside'.

Activity

- Take two pieces of similarly coloured paper and ask children to notice and then describe the difference in shade. Initially the most obvious adjectives are acceptable – lighter, darker, a greener green, etc. Add a third piece of paper and encourage further discussion of difference. Add a fourth and fifth … Children will appreciate the increasing challenge but may start to struggle.
- Use a blank grid as in Figure 10.1, making sure it has more boxes than the number of usable ideas the children had for describing differences of colour. Decide how the

lighter

	lime green		dayglo green
grasshopper green			
	acorn green		
Yew tree green			

darker

more natural   less natural

Figure 10.1

descriptions will be organized by labelling the vertical and horizontal axes of the grid. So as Figure 10.1 shows you may pick 'darker to lighter' and 'more natural to less natural' (i.e. more fluorescent).
- Discuss where the different descriptive words and phrases will fit on the grid, using the basic parameters (dark/light, natural/artificial) as a guide.

Learning benefits

- Gives children experience in noticing fine distinctions (in this case between colours) and searching for words that articulate their observations.
- Encourages wordplay – i.e. making new word combinations. This helps to break the habit of choosing 'off the peg' descriptions such as jet black, sea green, blood red, etc.
- Further familiarizes children with the function and range of adjectives and adjectival phrases.

Practical tips

- Help children to generate more choices by playing the noun-to-adjective game. An obvious example is to take the noun 'lime' and use it descriptively – lime green. Get the children to make a list of green objects and create descriptive terms out of it. They will rediscover familiar phrases like bottle green but will come up with some delightful new ideas too – one boy invented 'school tie green'. Another thought of 'almost-blue-green'. Also try matching colours with moods or feelings. Ask the group what envious green would look like, or bitter green, relaxed green, happy green.

- Another technique is to append another colour to (in this case) green and then ask children to describe it in more detail. They will be familiar with a phrase like bluey-green, but how might they describe purply-green, reddish-green, yellowy-green?

Taking it further

- Approach the task through similes. Use the template *as green as ...* and ask the group to complete the simile for each shade you show them. Ideas from groups I've worked with include:
  - as green as a waist-deep lagoon
  - as green as a lawn in late August
  - as green as the first leaf of spring
  - as juicy green as a big bite of cucumber (this is an interesting one as it makes a 'sensory crossover' with taste and texture).

32 GETTING STARTED

We look at similes again on pages 41–3.

- All of this work aims to encourage children to 'reach for more words' in describing subtle differences they've noticed. Extend the activity by showing the group a paint colour chart. These are usually free from DIY stores or you can easily grab them from the Internet. If the colours on the chart are named, ask children to investigate any terms they don't understand. In the phrase 'burnt sienna' for instance, what is sienna? If they come across 'terracotta red', suggest they get hold of a piece of terracotta and check it against the colour on the chart. Another activity is to cut out the various shades of one colour and have children place the cut-outs into the colour grid you created earlier.

SECTION 2
Building Narrative

CHAPTER 11

Prediction Strips

Activity 1

You can use this activity to consolidate some of the techniques explained earlier.

Cut strips of pictures from the grids on pages 102–12, or cut individual images to create new picture strips. Alternatively ask children to make up the strips themselves: it's not necessary for them to deliberately think of a story at this point. If the children create the resource, have them swap sequences with each other.

The basic 'prediction strip' activity asks children to decide what story the picture sequence is telling, then to think about what might happen next. This can be accomplished in several ways:

1. Add another strip to the end of the first as a way of suggesting how the story continues.

2. Working as a group: a child adds one image to the end of the sequence and the group discusses how that takes the story on. A second child adds another image and further discussion follows. Continue adding images one at a time until the story is 'rounded off' and completed.

3. Create a long strip with images filling the first four or five boxes, followed by several blank boxes, then an image in the last box. Decide what story is being told by the images early in the sequence. If the last image said something about how the story ends, what events lead up to that? In other words, what would fill the empty boxes? Children can either find pictures that fit, or simply discuss and decide upon the finished narrative.

4. **Many Endings**: Create strips with pictures at the front followed by blank boxes. Split the children into groups. Designate other children as 'scribes', enough for one per group. Each group takes a picture strip and works out what would fit in the blank boxes, i.e. how the story continues. The scribe makes a note of their decision, then takes the strip on to another group where the activity is repeated. Eventually every group will have looked at all the strips, while each strip will have a number of endings attached to it. This activity brings home very powerfully to children that there is no one right way to build a narrative. Events follow on one from another in a reasoned way, and the author is making decisions constantly about which 'route' through a story works best.

5   A variation of the 'Many Endings' game is for any one group to keep the same strip. Then someone from that group picks up a single image or short strip prepared earlier. Discussion follows about how the story might develop. Then the end strip is discarded and another strip picked up so that a different ending can be created. The group does this a number of times to create several possible endings. Discussion then follows to decide which ending works best.

Learning benefits

- Demonstrates that children have choice and control in their storymaking.
- Develops reasoning ability.
- Raises awareness of the 'principle of potential', that even a small number of simple images can be manipulated in many ways and so have the potential to generate a large number of ideas.

Activity 2

The Ongoing Story. Obtain some blank till rolls (readily available in most stationery stores). Get the children to cut out plenty of images and prepare themselves for a marathon challenge:

- Pick a few images that kickstart a story. Glue them to the start of the till roll. Keep selecting images to stick to the roll as you continue to work on the story. You've finished either when the story seems completed or when you run out of pictures. If there's room, write a summary of the story below the long line of pictures on the till roll.

- Stick a long line of images on the roll. There's no need to think of a story at this stage. Roll up the roll and swap with another person. Take the new roll you've just been given, begin to unroll it, and see if you can make up a story that uses all of the images. Tip: You might find it easier to create your story verbally rather than write it down at this stage.

Learning benefit

This activity helps children to feel more comfortable with what's called 'stream of consciousness' writing. This is a useful technique because it dampens down the tendency some children have to struggle to think of ideas and/or to 'over think' them.

> **Practical tip**
>
> The aim of the game is simply to keep going, making up a more-or-less reasonable narrative as the line of images unrolls. This can also work well as a small group activity where participants' ideas feed into each other.

Activity 3

Story Envelopes. Each group is given an envelope and a genre grid of their choice. Images are cut out and arranged in a line as a simple story is made up. The story or a summary of it is written on a piece of paper small enough to fit unfolded into the envelope. Put the story summary and images into the envelope, write the genre on the outside and pass it to another group that would like to make a story in the same genre. Then the process is repeated, so that eventually each envelope contains several story summaries, together with the images that were used to compose them.

> **Taking it further**

You can extend this activity by allowing children to create new images on scraps of paper, which they can incorporate into the story envelope game.

> **Learning benefit**
>
> Using this simple linear way of storymaking prepares children for working with more complex narrative structures, explored later.

CHAPTER 12

Connectives

Connectives give a narrative chain of events cohesion and variety. You can help children to familiarize themselves with a range of connectives and use them more flexibly by using various story strand techniques.

We've already come across the use of connectives in Contextualizing and Interpreting (Chapter 4). Here's a way of building on that.

Activity 1

- Arrange a number of concentric circles on a large sheet of paper.
- Cut out a number of images from one or more grids and place one in the middle circle.
- Explain to the group that you'll be playing the 'while game' first. Let's suppose you've chosen images from the pirate grid on page 109 and placed the pirate in the middle of the nested circles (see Figure 12.1). Make up a sentence to set the game going, such as 'The pirate John Hawk was dreaming of buried treasure.' Then pick up another image – we'll use the word 'Board' and add it to the game by placing it on the next circle out and adding to the story. So, 'While John Hawk was dreaming of buried treasure some enemy pirates were sneaking on board his ship.' Invite a child to pick up another image to place on the next circle and build into the story:

Alysha: While enemy pirates were sneaking aboard John Hawk's ship, he remembered seeing an old map in a little shop near the harbour.
Luke: While John Hawk thought of the map, the enemy pirates set sail in his ship.
Evie: While the ship was sailing away, John Hawk noted which direction it was travelling in, then hurried to the shop to buy the map …

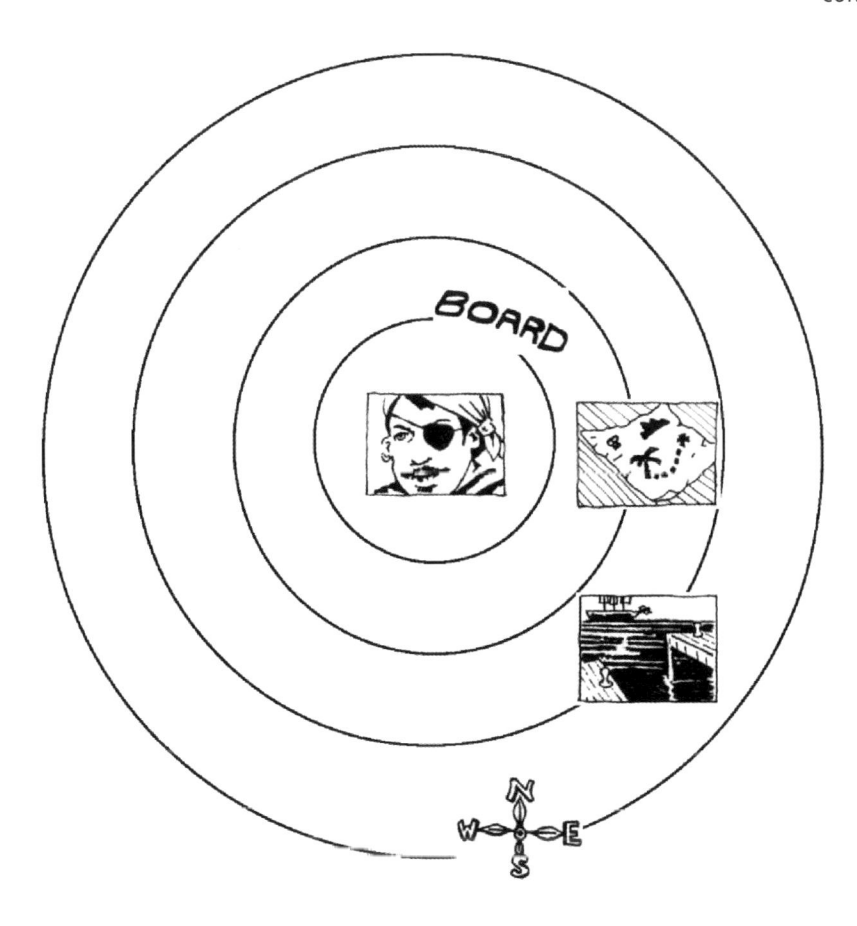

Figure 12.1

👍 Learning benefits

- The immediate value of this game is that it allows children to mentally 'roam spatially' within the story. Their imaginations, focused first on John Hawk, move easily then to the shop in the town, to the harbour, etc. This helps children to master the technique of third person writing. Sometimes a young writer is stuck in what I call partial-third-person, where the he/she voice is used, but where the child's imagination is fixed on one character throughout, not because the character needs to be the focus of the story at that point, but because the writer doesn't make a 'meanwhile-leap' to a different scene.

- The use of the nested circles also acts as a visual analogue for 'moving out' from the central starting point. It becomes a simple thing for a child to say, 'Meanwhile a thousand miles away the treasure lay buried on a desert island', and place a suitable image on one of the outer circles.

Activity 2

Another game gives practice in the use of many other connectives:

- Cut plenty of images from one or more grids and arrange them face up around the edge of a large sheet of paper.
- Prepare scraps of paper with a different connective written on each scrap (although you can repeat connectives if you wish). You might want to arrange the scraps in clusters for the various categories of connectives that exist:

    Adding: and, also, as well as, moreover, etc.
    Cause and effect: because, so, therefore, besides
    Qualifying: however, although, unless, except

    and so on. (See *http___www.lancsngfl.ac.uk_nationalstrategy_ks3_science_getfile.php_src=27_ Connectives* for a useful list.)

- What the children have now are lots of images and a range of connectives all available at a glance. Explain that the pictures and connectives will be arranged zig-zag style like the words on a page.
- Place a picture in the top left-hand corner of the working area and start the story off. 'The pirate John Hawk was chained up in a dungeon.' Children take turns to pick another image and connective, placing them in line as they build the narrative.

    Emily: However his friends were planning to rescue him.
    Michaela: Because only John knew where the treasure was buried.
    Misbah: As long as John was not moved to Prison Island his friends' plan might succeed.
    Christina: Therefore they decided to rescue him that night!

Learning benefits

The aim of this game is to raise children's awareness of the appropriate use of connectives. The story that emerges will probably sound a bit forced and artificial, self-consciously crammed as it is with connectives! Further work can knock off these rough edges and help children to understand that as with so many aspects of using language elegantly, the old Chinese wisdom applies: 'Use words as you would fry a small fish. Lightly.'

CHAPTER 13

Proverbs and Similes

Create the opportunity for children to discuss these and make up their own.

Activity 1

- The simplest game uses some well-known proverbs and images selected to illustrate them (children can draw their own if necessary). So 'a bird in the hand is worth two in the bush' would be written on a sheet and be accompanied by five images – a hand, a bird placed on or near it, a bush and two birds placed on or near that. The act of physically arranging the pictures and the visual reference they provide will help children to remember the proverbs more readily. Discussion about what the proverb means can follow.
- Once the meaning of the proverb has been agreed, invite children to pick different images to create variations. So for example:
  - A drowned rat in the harbour is worth two in the ship's hold (pirate grid).
  - A vampire prowling the night is worth two in the coffin [if you're another vampire that is!] (horror grid).
  - A sealed pyramid is worth two that have been looted (Egyptian grid).
- Create little visual scenarios to illustrate proverbs. Ask children what pictures they'd choose to 'tell the story' of the following …
  - No pain, no gain.
  - Oaks fall when reeds stand.
  - Set a thief to catch a thief.
  - The strength of the chain is the weakest link (goodbye!).

Practical tip

Note that children can draw their own pictures as necessary. Quite often creating such proverb scenarios leads young writers to think of more extended stories based on the initial idea.

Activity 2

Make-Your-Own-Proverb. This is a more difficult activity. The idea is to look at a genre grid and link two images to make a sentence that at least sounds like a proverb! So, here are some examples:

Pirate grid: When the rat is marooned on the island, the ship's biscuits last longer.
Science fiction grid: If the alien lands in your garden, a long journey is about to begin.
Animal adventure grid: The fox is never afraid of the scarecrow.

Learning benefits

- Children come to link concrete images to the often abstract principles behind proverbs.
- These activities act as a precursor to metaphorical thinking and the exploration of figurative expressions.
- Looking at proverbs can serve as a springboard into philosophical discussions and reasoned argument and debates (for more guidance, see for instance Bowkett 2009, *Countdown to Non-Fiction Writing* and Bowkett and Stanley 2004, *But Why?*)

Activity 3

Similes can be readily created by using the picture grids. Show the children one grid and offer a couple of similes you've made to illustrate the point. Using the pirate grid again:

As roguish as a pirate
As hopeless as a message in a bottle
As unpredictable as the four winds

Then use the brainstorm technique with the class to generate more. As ideas fade, change the grid and you'll probably get a fresh wave (as it were) of further ideas.

Learning benefits

Similes pave the way for children to understand metaphorical/figurative thinking. There's more about this on page 84. For now, consider the following activities.

Taking it further

- Use images on a chosen grid to investigate well-known expressions. For example, the picture of the scroll (or rolled up document) reminds me of scrolling down a page on a computer screen. What has 'scrolling' got to do with a scroll? On the same grid we also have 'a raft of ideas', 'a loose cannon', 'to coin a phrase' and 'draw a line in the sand'.

- Highlight the way that words can 'morph' into different parts of speech. So the noun 'treasure' becomes an adjective in 'a treasured possession'. The noun 'pirate' can become the verb 'to pirate' (illegally copy software and music). Even 'bottle' is used as the slang verb 'to bottle it'. Once children begin to get into the swing of this (oops, another metaphor) you can ask them to create new word-morphs, some of which will be startlingly fresh and original.

- Similes also achieve their effect by using the word *as* – as in 'as busy as a bee'. Again using the grids can familiarize children with the concept and throw up fresh and interesting ideas …
    - As unwashed as a pirate on a long voyage
    - As silent as bones in the desert
    - As exotic as sunset over the Pyramids
    - As cosy as a campfire

- Introduce other figurative expressions that can be illustrated with a picture from the grids, or an equally simple image that can be drawn. A simple list of such expressions and their meanings with pictures appended will help children to remember them:
    - Web (horror grid) – a web of lies
    - Blood (horror grid) – in cold blood
    - Triangle (romance grid) – a love triangle
    - Janus figure (romance grid) – two-faced
    - Bullet (wild west grid) – to bite the bullet
    - Fruit (animal grid) – the fruit of one's labours

- Make a more challenging game by preparing lots of cut out images. Lay them face down on a table. Have two teams. The first team turns up an image at random and the other team must think of a figurative expression, simile or proverb based on it. These can be well known or invented. Award more points to the invented ones. If the team that is challenged succeeds they earn points and the image is removed. The game proceeds by looking at images turn and turn about. If a team cannot think of a simile the opposing team gains a point and the image can either be removed or turned face down so that it will appear later. Doing this means that if a child has an idea in the meantime they'll have another chance to win points.

CHAPTER 14

Back Story

Young writers can make difficulties for themselves by restricting their thinking to a rigid beginning–middle–end pattern for a story. We often see this in stories that are quite mundane at the start as the scene is set (often with too much and/or unnecessary detail), with an exciting event – the 'real' start – happening half a page or more later. So there might be a lengthy explanation of the ordinary things Simpson did that morning before Malone sent him to fetch the money (see page 45). This is one reason why we encourage children to have 'good strong beginnings', and yet some still struggle to achieve this as they find it hard to break out of that linear-sequential way of thinking we've taught them – and which *finished* stories mirror.

Techniques for helping to overcome this include use of flashbacks, back story and overview.

Activity 1

Flashbacks. A flashback is a narrative device for jumping back in time to make mention of something that happened earlier. It can take the form of a single sentence – 'Luckily Simpson had memorized the combination of the safe when he'd seen Henderson put the money in there a week earlier.' Or an entire chapter or chapters might take us away from the here-and-now of the story to some point in the past, in which case it becomes more of a 'back story' (see below).

One way of teaching the use of flashbacks is to prepare a story strip as explained earlier. As children do this encourage them to leap straight into the action/some exciting situation. So for instance, Henderson is pursuing Simpson and Malone down a dangerously winding mountain road. He wants his money back.

Make that the opening scene. But of course the reader will want to know what happened to create that situation in the first place. In this case, ask the child to prepare a separate strip (using images and/or written notes in the boxes) which tells that part of the tale (see Figure 14.1).

Discuss where this strip might be inserted so as not to interrupt the pace and excitement of the main action. The result might end up as in Figure 14.1.

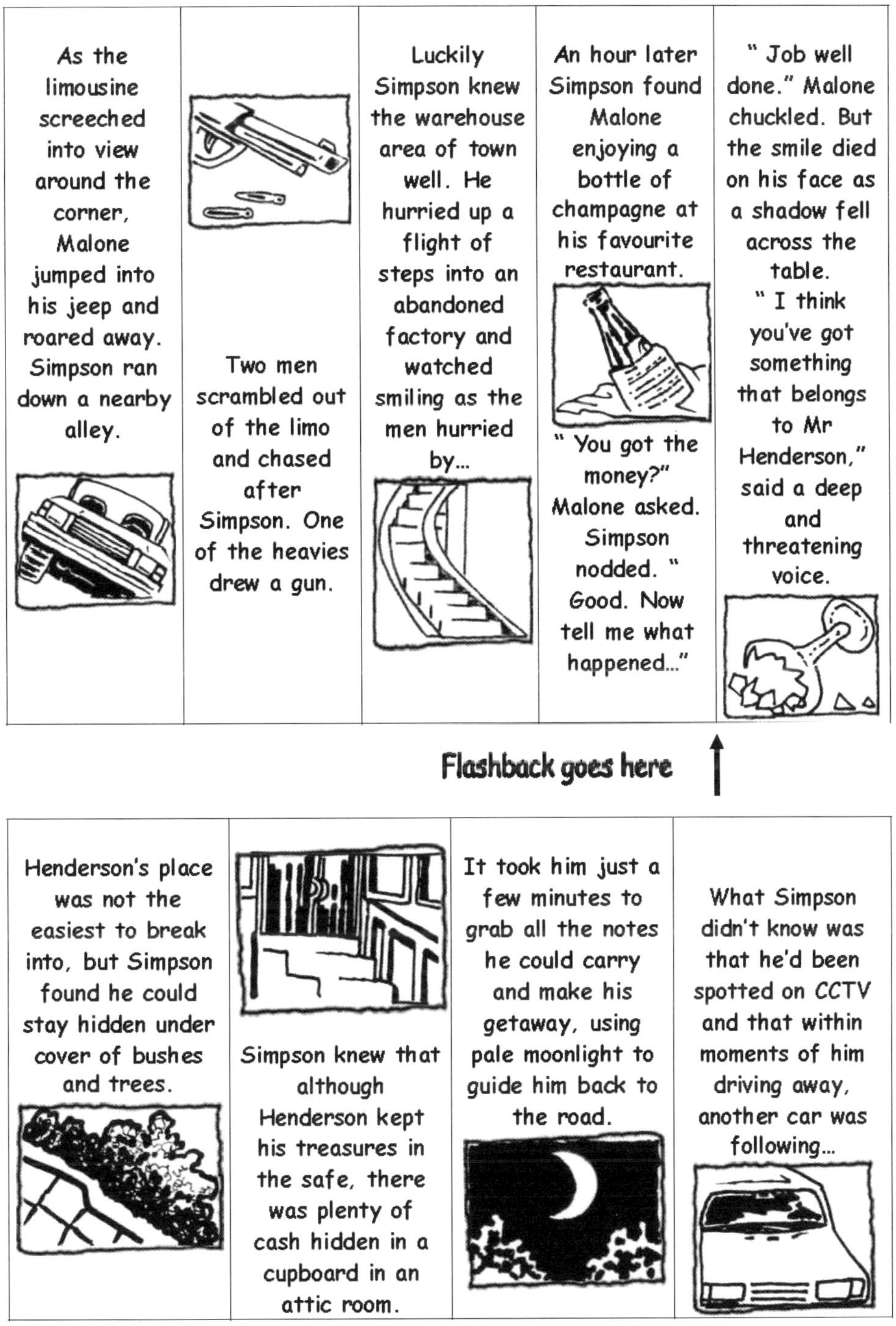

BACK STORY   45

| As the limousine screeched into view around the corner, Malone jumped into his jeep and roared away. Simpson ran down a nearby alley. | Two men scrambled out of the limo and chased after Simpson. One of the heavies drew a gun. | Luckily Simpson knew the warehouse area of town well. He hurried up a flight of steps into an abandoned factory and watched smiling as the men hurried by... | An hour later Simpson found Malone enjoying a bottle of champagne at his favourite restaurant. "You got the money?" Malone asked. Simpson nodded. "Good. Now tell me what happened..." | "Job well done." Malone chuckled. But the smile died on his face as a shadow fell across the table. "I think you've got something that belongs to Mr Henderson," said a deep and threatening voice. |

Flashback goes here ↑

| Henderson's place was not the easiest to break into, but Simpson found he could stay hidden under cover of bushes and trees. | Simpson knew that although Henderson kept his treasures in the safe, there was plenty of cash hidden in a cupboard in an attic room. | It took him just a few minutes to grab all the notes he could carry and make his getaway, using pale moonlight to guide him back to the road. | What Simpson didn't know was that he'd been spotted on CCTV and that within moments of him driving away, another car was following... |

Figure 14.1

Activity 2

Back Story. The term 'back story' indicates a more substantial chunk of narrative that explains past events so that the reader is 'brought up to speed' with what is happening now. Sometimes a back story forms an entire story in its own right, a 'prequel' to the central narrative.

Most children will never or rarely attempt to build a story in that much detail (although I have met very keen young writers who are up for the challenge!) Simply introducing the term is usually sufficient, but if a child wants to attempt a back story then the use of picture strips as used for flashbacks might prove useful. In this case the 'flashback strip' would form a completed narrative in its own right, and would be written up as a separate story.

Activity 3

Overview. This is simply the trick of helping children to summarize a cluster of details in a single general statement. Sometimes the same linear-sequential style of thinking that makes it hard for young writers to jump right in to the action of a story makes them want to explain everything to the same degree of detail. Often a simple overview statement will do the job more effectively, since it doesn't slow the story's pace. So instead of describing in detail Simpson's adventures in retrieving the money for Malone, one might just say 'Simpson cleverly avoided all the traps Henderson set and had the money in his hands within an hour.'

Children will have come across the technique of 'overviewing' if they looked at the summarizing activities on pages 11–13. Now they are working with more details. A quick way of practising this is to use story strips that children have completed earlier. Ask one child to tell their story in as much detail as they like, using the picture strip as a prompt. Then ask others in the group to write one sentence saying what the story is basically about. So for the example we've been using – Malone, a criminal mastermind, sends his henchmen out to steal money from rich victims.

Learning benefits

- Begins to break the habit of the rigidly linear structure 'beginning–middle–end', allowing children to build more variety and flexibility into their narratives.
- Paves the way for more sophisticated narrative devices such as story arcs (plot threads spanning more than one story), prequels, sequels and linking themes.

CHAPTER 15

Story 'Ingredients'

I use this term to mean events and situations that influence the emotional tone of the story and thus the reader's emotional response. The culinary metaphor is deliberate. So for instance, I explain to children that *violence* is like a hot chilli powder and it doesn't take much to ruin the flavour of the dish. *Humour* too is a potent spice, although it can be used in greater quantity if the story is intentionally a comedy. The notion of emotions-as-spices allows us to extend the metaphor to talk about blending ingredients, flavouring a story, lacing, drizzling, ladling, spooning and so on. The analogy of measuring quantities implies that young writers can and should have a degree of control over what goes into the pot.

Activity

- You can use images from the grids to get the point across. First assemble a list of the kinds of ingredients that help to make stories interesting – tension, danger, fear, action-drama, violence, humour, etc.

- Now select an image or a short sequence of images. Let's suppose we choose the little drawing of hills we've used before. Say to the group 'Who can think of a situation that happens in the hills and features – danger.' Record responses then move on. 'Using the same picture, who can think of a situation that would make the reader feel uneasy?' And so it goes on.

Learning benefits

- Offers a way of understanding and controlling the emotional aspects of a story and links them with the pace and tone of the writing.
- Emphasizes that creative writing is and should be an enjoyable emotional experience for both reader and writer.

Taking it further

You can extend the activity by making two sets of cards (or pieces of paper), one featuring ingredients and the other pictures from the grids. Shuffle both packs and lay them face down. Take a card from each pack and show them to the children taking part. So you might get bird + humour. How could these be combined in a story? Either collect all of the ideas that are generated or turn it into a competitive game, where the first child or group to make a reasonable link earns a point.

CHAPTER 16

Cliffhangers

Most children I meet have learned about the cliffhanger. This narrative device ends the scene or chapter at a dramatic moment, leaving the reader wanting more. Like many techniques in writing this one works well if it is not over-used. Also, it's important to remember that a cliffhanger becomes unsatisfying if the story is not properly resolved and if all loose ends are not tied up.

Activity

Practise 'cliffhanging' by showing the group suitable images to generate edge-of-your-seat sentences, as in Figure 16.1.

Point out some of the tricks that help to create the dramatic effect you're looking for:

- Words and phrases that spring a surprise or emphasize speed – suddenly, unexpectedly, without warning.
- Exclamations – Look out! Duck! Oh no it's happening!
- Use of the ellipsis, which is the omission of words whose presence would complete the sense of the sentence. The missing words are indicated by (…) – And then …, It was only a matter of time before …, The shadow loomed out of the darkness behind Joe …
- Strong verbs and verb phrases – lights blazed, the jeep slewed, rocks tumbled.
- Exaggeration (to be used sparingly) – half the cliff came tumbling towards them.
- Use of the en dash (–) which creates a kind of 'leap' to a revelation – It was true – he really could see into people's minds!
- Vivid details – eyes of startling blue, a single drop of bright red blood splashed onto the white pillow, the sound pierced like a needle.
- Vagueness to create a sense of mystery and unease – the mysterious stranger, something moved among the bushes, Andrea noticed a flicker of movement out of the corner of her eyes.

50 BUILDING NARRATIVE

 *[rockfall image]*	• Suddenly there was a rumbling sound. The explorers looked up and saw half the cliff tumbling towards them. • "Look out!" Johansen cried, "it's an avalanche!" • Slowly the dust settled after the rockfall, but there was no sign of Tim and Tina…
 *[jeep image]*	• Lights blazed. The jeep swung into view and came bearing down upon them. • Without any warning the steering went light and the vehicle slewed over towards the edge of the cliff. • It was the dead of night. No-one woke to the sound of petrol dripping underneath the car, nor the soft *whoosh* moments later as the fuel caught fire.
 *[eye image]*	• The mysterious stranger had eyes of startling blue. Julia was quite hypnotised by them. "You summoned me," he said in a quiet voice. "And now you must face the consequences." • The robbery had gone without a hitch. Simpson stuffed the money in his pocket and hurried from the room – unaware that he was being watched by hostile eyes… • Ben was frightened. His eyes had felt funny, kind of itchy, all day. At first he hadn't believed it, but it was true – he really could see into people's minds!

Figure 16.1

Practical tip

The entire purpose of cliffhangers is to make the reader want to read on. Although cliffhangers can be big and dramatic effects, the technique can be used more delicately and on a smaller scale at the ends of scenes as a kind of mini-climax that 'primes the palate' for the next instalment.

Learning benefits

- Practising 'cliffhanging' gives young writers further control over the structure of a story by showing them how to influence pace and dramatic tension.
- It provides motivation for children who 'get bored' with their stories (often because nothing exciting is happening in the story at that point).

CLIFFHANGERS 51

Taking it further

Use the narrative line idea (see pages 56–9) and ask children to imagine it's like an old-fashioned clothesline strung between two poles. Ordinarily it would sag in the middle, but if clothes props are used the entire line is supported. Each peak along the line corresponds to a cliffhanger, as in Figure 16.2. Encourage children to build these into their stories at the planning stage.

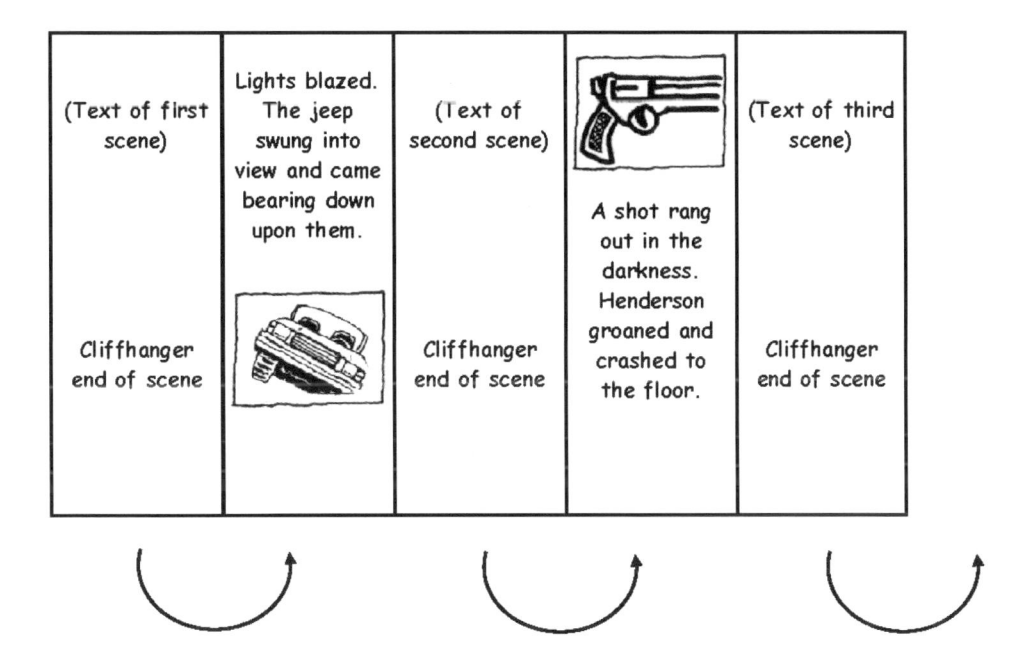

| (Text of first scene)

Cliffhanger end of scene | Lights blazed. The jeep swung into view and came bearing down upon them. | (Text of second scene)

Cliffhanger end of scene | A shot rang out in the darkness. Henderson groaned and crashed to the floor. | (Text of third scene)

Cliffhanger end of scene |

Figure 16.2

CHAPTER 17

The Neverending Story

Most children understand that a story moves through the phases of beginning (setting the scene/introducing characters/initiating action), middle (introducing complications/moving the action on) and end (resolution/tying up of loose ends/return to normality). Often young writers will use that word 'resolution' as they talk about the final phase of the narrative – but when I ask them what the word actually means I'm often met with vague replies or with silence.

I explain that all good stories are about a problem that has to be solved, although not so much solved as re-solved. The resolution is a 're-solution', a solving again of the kinds of problems that characters have had to deal with ever since stories were invented. And, because stories reflect real life and the human condition, resolutions have been happening since we became recognizably human – and I daresay even before that.

In talking about these things we approach a number of big ideas that go to the heart of what makes a story a story. The first of these ideas concerns what are sometimes called the basic narrative elements, which you can introduce to the children in your classroom.

Basic Narrative Elements: Heroes, Villains and …

The folklorist Vladimir Propp (see Propp 2001) has given us valuable insights into the basic elements or building blocks of narrative. Explain to the children that at its simplest a robust story will contain:

– **A hero**. This character represents noble qualities such as courage, kindness, altruism, self-sacrifice and so on. Although hero figures are not always whiter-than-white (the notion of the anti-hero being one aspect of this) they take risks in the service of others and often put others' needs above their own. Indeed, it was the mythologist Joseph Campbell who said that the difference between a hero and a celebrity is that a hero helps others and a celebrity helps himself. It's also important to realize that heroes – sometimes the most engaging – are just ordinary people whose qualities don't emerge until they meet extreme circumstances and are tested to the limit. By the same token heroes are often vulnerable and have flaws and weaknesses that ultimately make their heroism more believable and memorable.

– **A villain**. The boo-hiss figure is central to a good story and represents the 'mean' qualities of selfishness, greed, desire to control and most of the other things the hero is not. But again, believable villains tend not to be characters of pure evil. In explaining this to children

I show them the ancient symbol of the Yin-Yang, Figure 17.1. The white part represents the hero, but within the white there is a patch of blackness. Likewise the blackness of the villain is relieved by the existence of a white dot. Notice too how the two opposing halves are intertwined to create the rounded whole: the hero and villain *need each other*. Without one the other would have no purpose or even existence. Also implicit in the Yin-Yang symbol is the idea of dynamic tension. The hero and villain are in an eternal struggle. The villain seeks to upset the balance of life, the hero to restore it. To illustrate this I say that St George will never truly be vanquished, but the dragon will never be finally slain. This is why in narrative (and perhaps in life too) there is no final solution, only re-solutions of problems that keep appearing as a natural consequence of our existence. In helping children to understand villains I invoke the things-happen-for-reasons rule and will not allow a villain to be simply 'bad because he is' or mentally deranged. Explaining a villain's actions because he is mad is an easy way out and amounts to lazy thinking. Apart from that psychotic villains are rarely believable. To make them convincing is difficult and a challenge to the author's skill that many children are reluctant to take up.

Figure 17.1

- **A problem**. Every story has a central problem, which the hero and others 'on his side' must resolve. The villain and his cohorts usually cause the trouble, and every decent problem leads to complications that gives the story its pace and texture. Again, the problem needs to be believable within the context of the story. The psychotic villain who wants to destroy the world because his mother didn't love him just won't wash (the problem won't wash that is, not the villain). The problem here, as it were, is that we again have the because-he's-mad rationale, while the sheer scale of the villainy weakens the problem. 'The very fabric of the cosmos is at risk if we don't stop him!' is hokey and I try to dissuade children from using exaggeration or over-blown problems. Having said that, if a child will only write on this grand scale then I put on my tolerant hat and let it happen.
- **A journey**. The hero usually embarks on a journey to resolve the problem. This may be intertwined with a journey undertaken by the villain to thwart the hero's actions.

- Obviously we're talking of a physical journey across different terrains, but there is also a symbolic aspect to it as when people on reality TV shows say they have been 'on a journey', which is to say a testing but ultimately transformational experience.

- **A partner**. Giving the hero and/or the villain a partner naturally creates the opportunity for dialogue and subplotting. The partner can be sent away on a mission, which may be told through a direct change-of-scene, a flashback or a recounting. On a more 'mythic' level, the partner can also represent some suppressed, flawed or absent element of the hero/villain's psyche. So a cowardly partner matched with a brave and reckless hero can help the hero gain insights into his own mortality and the foolishness of his devil-may-care attitude. Partners also serve the function of sounding-boards for the hero/villain's opinions and explanations – 'I've kept my laboratory experiments a secret from everyone Igor, but I will reveal all to you now!'

- **A source of help**. This highlights the essential humanity and vulnerability of the hero. When the villain needs help we as readers can feel a surge of hope that he will not succeed in his evil schemes after all. Of course, the main characters can themselves be the source of help – ultimately that's the hero's function. When the hero helps his partner, that action serves to strengthen the bond between them. Help more generally can arrive in the form of other characters. Accident and happenstance can also be helpful, although the overuse of coincidence, and unbelievable coincidence, needs to be discouraged – 'Malone's gun was empty, but as he glanced despairingly at the floor he was amazed to see someone had dropped some bullets – exactly the ones he needed!' In Fantasy tales the gods look down on our mortal world (and the demons look up), and so here help can be of a supernatural nature.

- **Knowledge applied as power**. This often takes the form of the gaining and losing of the advantage. In other words the hero-and-friends have the upper hand, but then some disaster befalls them and the villain is on the ascendant. This is a temporary situation however and soon the hero gains the advantage over the villain. Using this element keeps the 'pot bubbling' (maybe that's where we get the idea of a pot-boiler of a story?). It's a technique used constantly in TV soaps, where gaining the upper hand by learning something useful operates in a complex way amongst the cast of characters.

- **A significant object**. This provides focus for the action of the story and offers a rationale for the characters' actions. The object may be something physical. Traditionally the object may need to be found and returned to its proper place, or destroyed. Sometimes the object is fragmented and the separate parts have to be found and integrated. The object may be more metaphorically the hero's efforts to resolve the problem – the object of his quest as it were.

Practical tip

When I introduce these elements to children I first ask them to think about a favourite story, book, film, comic strip or whatever. Then I show them 'Mr Propp's magic formula' and ask them to notice how many of the elements appear in the tale they've chosen.

Activity

Create a grid such as the one in Figure 17.2 and invite children to fill in the boxes. If you are interested in looking at these ideas in more detail, I recommend Stuart Voytilla's book *Myth and the Movies* (1999). Here Voytilla looks at a number of the most popular and influential movies of the past several decades and analyses them in terms of Propp's narrative elements and the 'narrative template', explained below.

	Hero	Villain	Problem	Journey	Partner	Help	K / P	Object
Harry Potter								
Lord of the Rings								
Tracey Beaker books								
Etc...								

Figure 17.2

Learning benefits

- Provides a robust template for creating a 'structurally sound' story in any genre.
- Gives children an analytical tool for studying other stories they read.
- Offers a strategy for planning. Instead of having an idea for a particular plot, children can build the narrative 'from the bottom up' by considering the basic elements of story first.

CHAPTER 18

The Narrative Template

The narrative line of beginning–middle–end, which at its simplest is a straight line, can be redrawn as in Figure 18.1 to show the fundamental shape of a story, the basic narrative template. After reading the notes below introduce the ideas at an appropriate point to increase the children's understanding of how stories are constructed.

∞

Figure 18.1

Imagine that the left-hand loop represents the hero's ordinary world and day-to-day life. The right-hand loop represents unfamiliar circumstances and places, extraordinary events and 'the territory of challenge and testing'. In traditional tales, myths and legends the two areas are sometimes called this world and the other world, or the familiar realm and the alien realm. The hero's journey can be mapped out along a number of strategic points, which mark significant events in or stages of the story (see Figure 18.2).

1 The story opens with the hero living his (or her) ordinary life. All's well with the world. Soon after there comes what is known as the *call to action*, where at least the first hint of the story's central problem is revealed. Traditionally the hero is reluctant to embark on the quest (for any number of reasons) but is persuaded to go, perhaps by others or through the voice of conscience.

2 This point is known as *heeding the call*. The hero commits himself to act, makes necessary preparations and sets out.

3 Soon there comes a *descent* into difficulty or danger. The pace of the story often picks up here as the excitement increases and the hero faces more and more challenging circumstances.

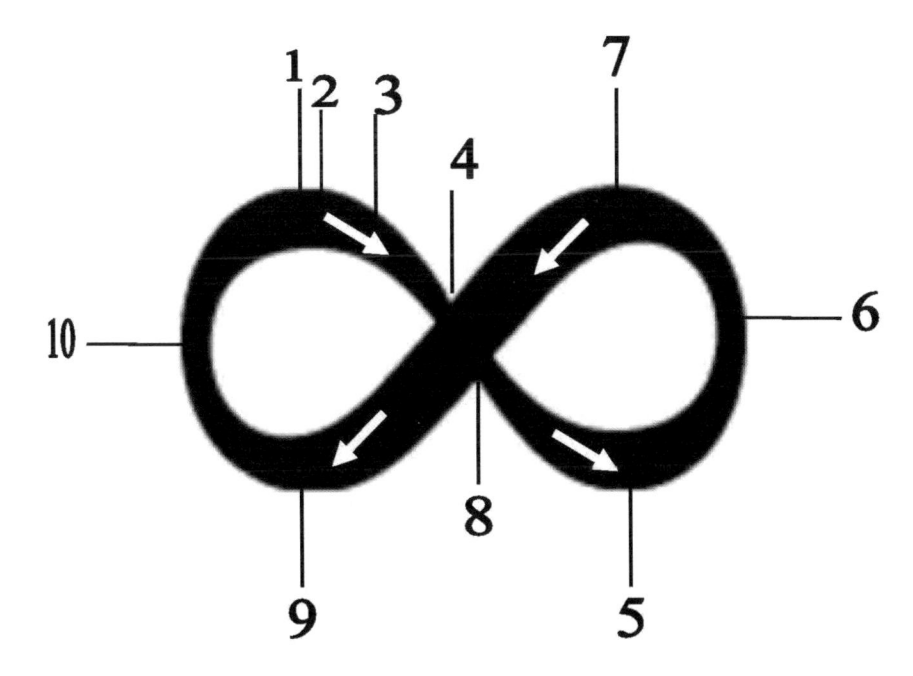

Figure 18.2

4 This is the *threshold*, where the hero crosses into unfamiliar territory and situations and is thrown back even more upon his own resources. In traditional tales the hero encounters here a figure known as the *threshold guardian*. This character may be a source of help or the first of the hero's 'big challenges' on his quest.

5 The hero encounters the *point of lowest ebb* where sometimes he feels things can't get worse and despair sets in. However because he *is* the hero he rises to the challenge and forges ahead.

6 The situation seems to be getting better, but at *the farthest point from home* the hero faces his greatest ordeal. At this point someone of lesser qualities would crumble, but the hero rallies and continues on the journey towards home and normality.

7 We might call this *the point of false optimism*. Things have been on the up-and-up and it's easy for the hero and his friends to become complacent and feel that the journey's nearing its end. But there is a further descent –

8 To a *recrossing of the threshold*. The same guardian figure may be encountered, or another character who further tests the hero's mettle. But perhaps sensing that he is leaving the alien realm behind, having survived and come through, the hero will now muster the last of his energy to battle on …

9 But there is often a *twist in the tale*: another plunge into difficulty and danger, a last challenge for the hero to face –

10 Before he *returns home*, transformed, with the problem resolved, the villain defeated and balance and normality restored. If a *sequel* is planned, there may be a final fleeting glimpse of a fresh problem that would cause the hero to set out on his journey once more. But that's another story.

58 BUILDING NARRATIVE

I've described the narrative template in general terms because it offers the writer flexibility within a structure. Although it is said that there are only seven basic stories in the world,[1] the narrative template accommodates endless variations.

> **Practical tip**
>
> Before moving on, you might consider how the template could be used to consolidate or extend some of the activities we looked at earlier.

Activity 1

Some children might find the narrative template in its 'looped' form a little complicated. Simplify the idea by straightening it out into a line and appending easier-to-understand labels to the significant points in the narrative, as in Figure 18.3. Placing a strip of blank boxes beneath it allows young writers to cut and paste their own pictures in the spaces and/or make notes of major events.

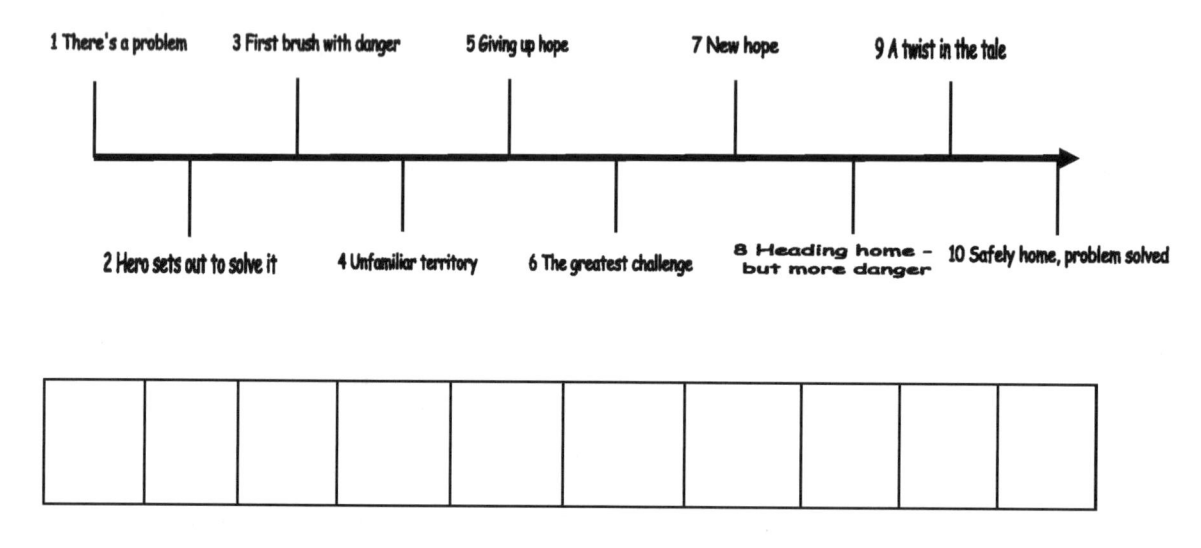

1 There's a problem 3 First brush with danger 5 Giving up hope 7 New hope 9 A twist in the tale

2 Hero sets out to solve it 4 Unfamiliar territory 6 The greatest challenge 8 Heading home – but more danger 10 Safely home, problem solved

Figure 18.3

Activity 2

Moebius Strip. Take a strip of paper, give it a half twist and sellotape the ends. The result is the Moebius (or Mobius) Strip, named after one recent discoverer of the idea, Ferdinand Mobius in 1858. A neat trick is to place the tip of a pen anywhere on the strip and draw a continuous line, i.e. without lifting the pen from the paper. Ultimately you will return to your starting point and discover the puzzling fact that the strip has only one boundary (see Figure 18.4).

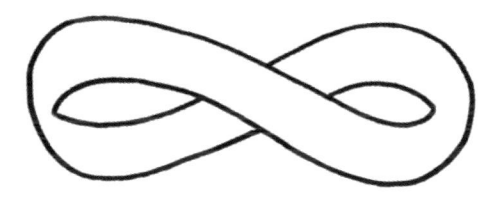

Figure 18.4

> ### 👍 Learning benefits
>
> - Shows how Propp's basic narrative elements are related to the overall structure of a story.
> - Helps children to build pace and dramatic tension into their writing.
> - Serves as an analytical tool for studying any story (in whatever medium – film, radio, play, etc.)

▶ Taking it further

Apart from being an entertaining trick, creating a Moebius Strip in the context of storymaking reinforces the universal nature of the narrative template (the same shape is, incidentally, the mathematical symbol for infinity). Apply the idea by creating a long picture strip (twenty or more images) and make a Moebius Strip out of it. Start at any picture and brainstorm a narrative with the class, attempting to round off the story as you return to your starting point (no need to try and use every single picture). Split the class into groups and give each one an identical strip. Have them start anywhere and go through the same activity. The chances are you'll end up with as many stories as there are groups.

Note

1 The aptly named Christopher Booker's (2007) monumental work, *The Seven Basic Plots*, explores this question in incredible detail, drawing as it does on a wealth of material from folktales and great works of literature to modern film and TV.

SECTION 3
Enriching the Story

CHAPTER 19

Parallel Story

Activity

- Do this as a whole-class activity: use the narrative template (Figure 18.2), or the simpler version (Figure 18.3), and create a story from a particular character's viewpoint. Accompany this with a picture strip, which can be made before, during or after you've worked out the narrative itself.

- Now split the class into groups and ask each group to retell the story from the viewpoint of one of the other characters – the villain, partner(s), threshold guardian, source of help, etc. Doing this requires some ingenuity. For instance, in the 'source narrative' (the original story) the villain's partner might never have met the hero, and yet this new parallel tale must be told from the villain's partner's perspective, obviously recounting the hero's adventures.

- In attempting a parallel story as much of the original story as possible must be retained, although new scenes can be added, reported by another character, etc., to fulfil the requirement. Any parallel story can be written in the first or third person.

- Once a number of parallel stories have been created, make picture strips for each. The strips will feature some images from the original tale, but also different ones in line with each character's unique perspective.

Learning benefits

- Further develops flexibility of thinking in the construction of narrative.
- Demonstrates the principle of potential (see page 11).
- Helps children to explore characters in more detail.
- Encourages the exploration of different writing styles (first and third person writing, various emotional tones depending on a character's viewpoint).

Taking it further

Vary the parallel story activity by introducing different forms of writing. For instance, could the story be told via an exchange of letters? Or as a diary, or in radio play format? (For more detail on forms, see my *Countdown to Creative Writing*, 2008.)

CHAPTER 20

Story Board Games

Activity

Images from the grids can easily be made into board games. Children can copy the templates, rules and mode-of-play of well-known games, or may be able to invent their own. The example in Figure 20.1, *Journey Through Space*, is a simple first-past-the-line race using motifs from Science Fiction. The basic board layout can be used with images from any genre however.

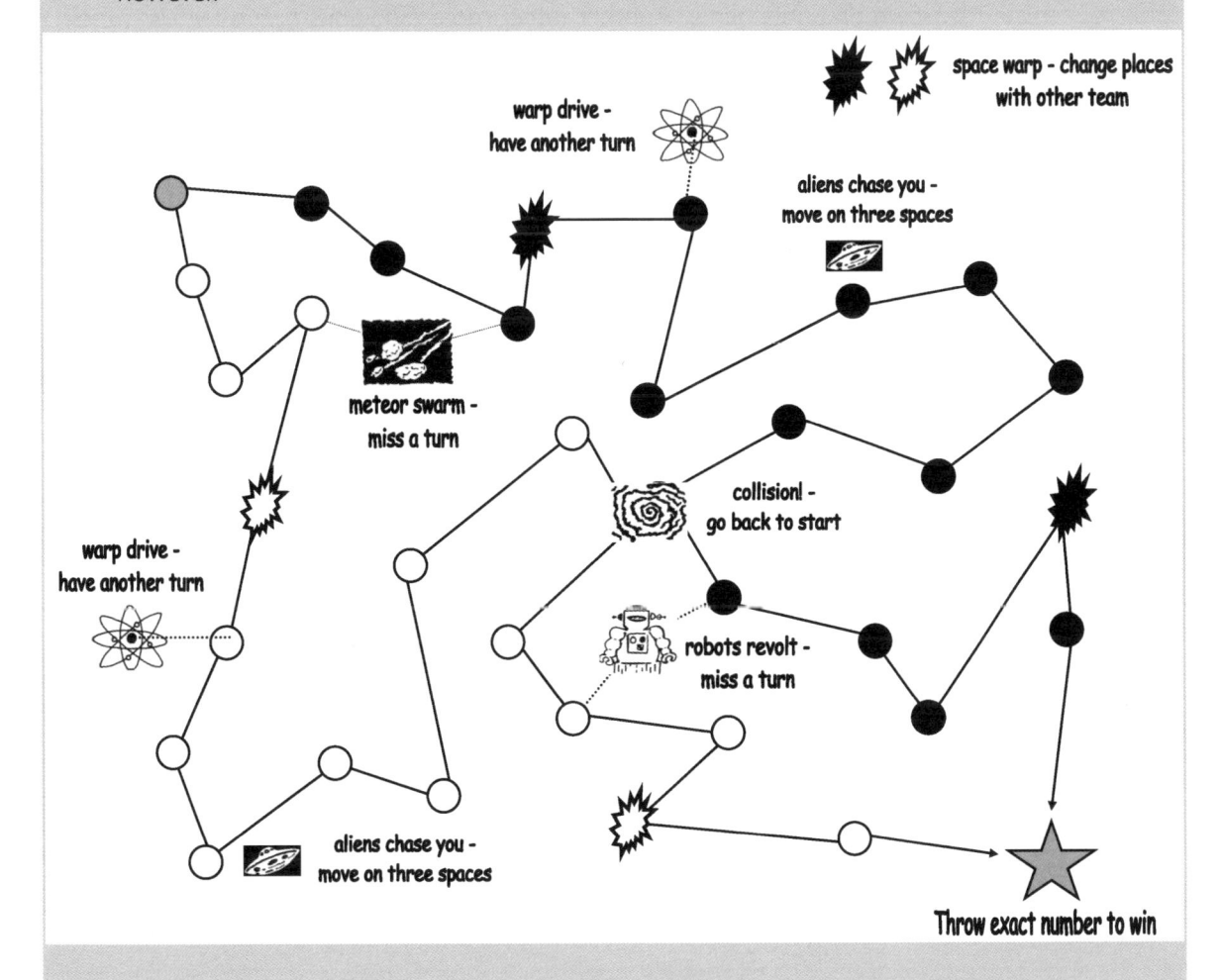

Figure 20.1

You can find a more complex example on the Web resource that accompanies this book. *The Search for the Kay-to-Bah Diamond* is set out in snakes-and-ladders fashion (though without the ladders and snakes!). You'll see that apart from hopefully being an enjoyable game to play, *Kay-to-Bah* also incorporates thinking games, word puzzles and other activities that are intended to have some learning value.

Practical tips

Board games that the children make can be based on the examples given and are easy to simplify. Versions I've come across include:

- Groups use the same game board but think of new puzzles and challenges.
- Create a new game board featuring a different genre and either modify the puzzles from *The Search for the Kay-to-Bah Diamond* or think of new ones.
- Use some of the images and puzzles given and build them into a new game board design (for instance Ludo or Monopoly). One group I worked with used the images to create their own draughts game. Another rather more ambitious group ran with the idea and opposing chess sets, by simply sticking images on to squares of card that could be used on a standard board.

A blank template (just the dotted routes) also appears below (Figure 20.2) and can also be downloaded from our website, but similar boards can easily be created in Word by using the autoshapes and line tools, WordArt for text, and then by importing pictures. It's likely that many children know even more ways of doing it! Alternatively images can be cut out and glued on to photocopied game boards – it's ideal if they can be copied A3 or larger, giving plenty of room for writing. Pictures can also be coloured in for effect.

Learning benefits

Making Story Board Games

- creates a context for instructional writing
- offers an opportunity for children to practise computer skills
- can serve as a means of generating ideas for stories, and acts as a planning device to test out aspects of the plot in game form first.

STORY BOARD GAMES 67

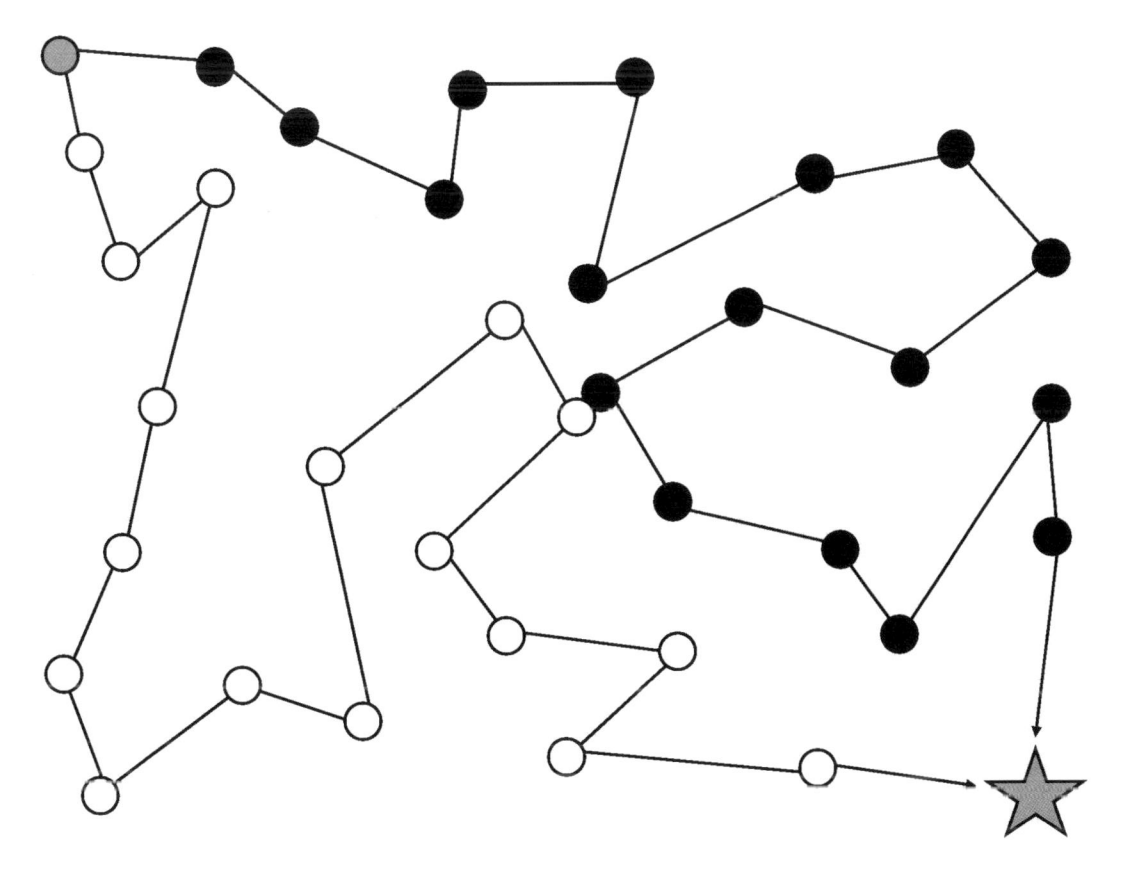

Figure 20.2

Taking it further

- Invite groups to choose from among the genre grids to create different games using the standard template.
- Provide vocabulary lists for children to incorporate into the game – see the note on 'the vocabulary of the subject' on page 95.
- Encourage groups to create board games based on stories they've read/listened to. In one school I visited a number of groups cut up comics to make superhero games, using their knowledge of the characters to create rules, traps, etc., within the context of the heroes' (and villains') powers.
- Have children create board games based on stories that they themselves have written – or work it the other way round and use the creation of such games to help children organize their ideas as they plan a subsequent piece of writing.
- Suggest to children that the exciting situations, crises and action sequences they put in their games can quite easily be transferred to their stories. If groups swap games not only will they experience a range of genres but also a variety of useful scenarios they can subsequently write up.

CHAPTER 21

Sequels

While motivating children to write can be a problem, sometimes there's no stopping them. I quite frequently meet young writers who announce (often shyly when no one else is listening) that they're 'doing a novel' and are already on Chapter 6 – or more. Sometimes in fact the novel has been finished and they're working on the sequel. The word itself comes from the Latin 'to follow' and sequels usually make use of a cast of characters, a theme or an ongoing situation to continue the saga. The fact that a writer has already done the hard work of thinking about these earlier, and realized them in the first story, means that a sequel can take shape quickly.

Doing some work on cliffhangers (pages 49–51) and chapter breakdowns, or the 'clothesline technique' (page 51) in narrative is further useful preparation for creating sequels. You might also try the following.

Activity 1

Make a list of prompts that help children to think beyond the first story. These might be suggested final sentences to the tale or indications of what might follow.

- But [name of hero] knew he had not seen the last of [name of villain].
- The danger was over – for now.
- So the secret was buried with him. [Name of hero] prayed it would stay that way.
- It was a year later. [Name of hero] thought she'd heard the last of [name of villain], but the unexpected telephone call proved her wrong.

Activity 2

Taking the Mind by Surprise. This is a technique we'll explore later in looking at the 6x6 grids. Engineering unexpected connections can kickstart the creative process and give children new ideas, in this case for sequels. Put some images in an envelope and as you ask the following questions or make the following statements (or similar) ask the child to take a picture out of the envelope to suggest an answer.

- What problem could the villain create this time?
- Where will the hero's next adventure take place?
- The picture you're about to look at will tell you something about the hero's (or villain's) partner in your sequel.[1]
- What big challenge will the hero face?
- Find out something about the 'threshold guardian'.

Alternatively, give the child the basic narrative template (page 56), take images at random from the envelope and lay them along the narrative path. What story is then suggested?

Activity 3

Take an image, either at random or the child can choose. Ask a closed (yes-no) question and flip a coin to force a choice. So using this image (Figure 21.1)
We might ask:

Figure 21.1

- Does the letter contain bad news?
- Is it the hero who receives the letter?
- Does this scene happen at the start of the story?
- Is there something valuable in the envelope?

And so on. Playing the coin-flip game means that the child ends up thinking 'unexpected thoughts' and exploring scenarios they might not otherwise have considered. It's true though that the game can lead to frustration if the young writer doesn't get their way. However, insist that they persevere until a useful amount of information has been gained. Then you can move on to the next stage . . .

Activity 4

If–Then Thinking. For every answer that the coin throws up, obviously another alternative remains unexplored. Go back and look at these unexamined possibilities. If the question was asked – Does the letter contain bad news? And the answer was no, subsequently go back and say 'But if it did, then . . .' How would the narrative grow out of that? If originally the child *wanted* the letter to contain bad news then they may well already have ideas about it in mind. Or begin with that 'yes, bad news' scenario and do some coin flipping to see where it takes you.

Activity 5

Many Endings – New Beginnings. The many endings game (page 35) can also be used to suggest storylines for sequels. Make new picture strips that have some connection with a story already written. Lay them out face down and have the child turn one over. 'If this was a follow-on story, what's happening?' Brainstorm ideas, then turn over another strip, either to suggest a different sequel or to tell you more about the sequel indicated by the first strip.

Learning benefits

These activities

- encourage active (exploratory) questioning as a planning tool
- raise awareness of the 'things happens for reasons' principle and gives practise in developing strong rationales. This increases the logical consistency of a story.

Note

1 The trick of saying 'this picture tells you something about . . .' is called *artful vagueness*. You've suggested your expectation that the child will succeed in learning something (in this case about the partner), but just what is still unknown. Taking the mind by surprise then prompts creative connections for the learning to happen. We'll look at this again in working with the grids and in developing characters (pages 82–4).

CHAPTER 22

Annotated Margins

Activity 1

- Ask the children to place images from the grids into the margin of their writing book. If they are still at the planning stage of the story, they can either have the pictures 'loose' in the margin, or fix them temporarily with Blu-tack. Suggest that children use the pictures as a focus for that part of the story, moving them as their ideas develop. The pictures can be spaced to suggest the pace of the plot. So for instance, if there is a fast-moving action sequence, a few pictures can be placed close together so that the writing about them takes up only a few lines. If a couple of characters are having quite a long conversation, pictures that illustrate what they are talking about can be chosen and spaced to fit how long the dialogue is to be. Other ways of annotating the margin with images are:

- Gluing images that shows the main sequence of events into the margin. These act as an aid to recall for summarizing and/or retelling the story.

- Once a story is written, ask the children to take out certain sections but place pictures in the margins that suggest what the missing portions are about. Have the children swap books and attempt to create the missing scenes.

- If you've run the parallel story activity with your class (pages 63–4), ask children to make up the picture strip again, but this time vertically, again spacing the pictures to follow the pace of the story. Ask them to paste the picture strip into the margin of a sheet of writing paper and write the story (or just make notes) from one character's point of view. Now give each child or group another sheet, place it to the left of the strip and write the same story, but from another character's viewpoint. See Figure 22.1.

Activity 2

Ask children to choose images and stick them into the margin of a partner's writing book over a few pages. Then the books are swapped back and each child uses the partner's selection of images as a prompt for creating their own story.

72 ENRICHING THE STORY

And you can keep going!

←

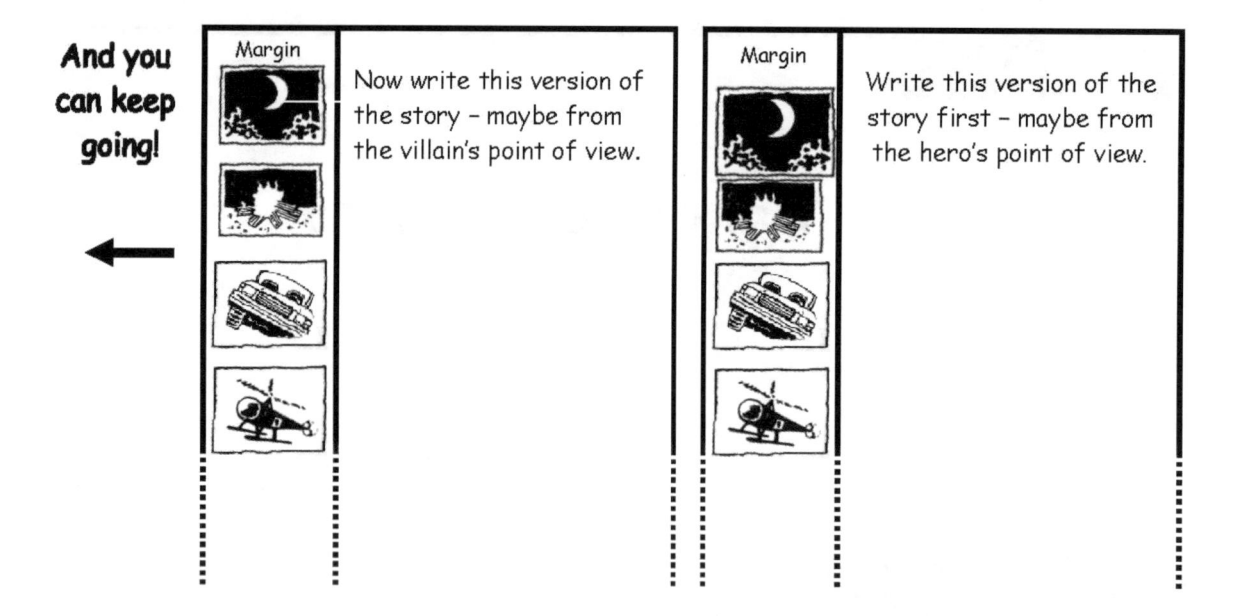

| Margin | Now write this version of the story – maybe from the villain's point of view. |

| Margin | Write this version of the story first – maybe from the hero's point of view. |

Figure 22.1

👍 Learning benefits

- Creates further opportunity for manipulating narrative.
- Offers creative challenges for storymaking.

23 Story Cards

Activity

This is a simple technique for helping children to 'open the doorway' into a story. Give each child a standard file card (12 $\frac{1}{2}$ × 7 $\frac{1}{2}$ cm or 5" × 3" works well); ask them to stick an image into the top left hand corner, then use it as a prompt to write a 'tempting intro', as in Figure 23.1. The outcome is particularly effective if the writing

- is in the second person (the 'you' voice)
- is in the present tense
- uses multisensory references (visual, auditory, tactile)
- ends with a 'hook' that encourages the child to write on.

This activity in itself requires minimal writing but a good deal of thought. Children can then either continue their own story or swap with a friend.

You and three friends are exploring an old house on the edge of town. You've heard rumours that it's haunted. You climb in through a broken window and stand in the dark and dusty hallway. The place smells of mould and damp.

Two of you decide to look around downstairs. You and your friend will explore the first floor. You climb the stairs, nervously shining the flashlight ahead. Suddenly the door of the upstairs room starts to creak open...

Figure 23.1

Practical tip

The pictures can be coloured in for effect. If you then laminate the results you have a permanent resource of around thirty cards to use with other groups.

Learning benefits

- Raises awareness of person and tense as aspects of creative writing.
- Gives practice in creating 'strong' openings for stories.

Taking it further

- Put a story card in the middle of a large sheet of paper and ask children to brainstorm further ideas. Use the Big Six question words and coin flips to generate information.

- Suggest that groups create a sequence of story cards, having roughly planned the whole story first. Each card can be a springboard into a scene or chapter. Such a sequence provides structure and plenty of ideas for the same or another group to complete the story subsequently.

- Help children to master the craft of writing by helping them to 'translate' second person story cards (or indeed entire stories) into the third or first person.

- Take a previously written story – a child's or one by a published author – and use it to create one or more story cards. When you give such cards to children who don't know the original work they are likely to write intriguingly different tales.

- **Two-Minute Tales**. Use both sides of a file card. Stick an image in the top left-hand corner on one side of the card and a second image in the bottom right-hand corner on the other side. These suggest the beginning and ending of a (very) short story that the child is invited to write on the card. Note that some children prefer to draft the tale on a separate sheet before polishing and then rewriting it on the card.

- Choose your own adventure cards. The idea is based on the popular books first published in the 1980s, where a story is broken down into a number of segments that trace several possible routes through the tale (see Jackson and Livingstone 2002). At key points the reader/character is asked to make a decision that determines which route they will take. If the reader makes a wrong decision and/or 'dies' in the story, they can go back and try again.

    Children might like the challenge of creating their own choose-your-own adventures. Each story segment can be written on a card. Care must be taken that the cards offer crossover points to the different routes through the tale and fit within the context of the whole story.

- **Chain Story**. Someone starts the chain by making a basic story card that covers the first scene or paragraph of the story. The card is passed on. The second writer chooses a suitable image and continues the tale on another story card, then passes that on. Once children have created such a chain story they may well be keen to break their own record next time.

- **Mini Sagas**. A mini saga is a story of *exactly* fifty words, but you are also allowed a title of up to six words. The main learning benefit of setting this task is that it's good for sharpening up children's editing skills. Many young writers (and adults too who try this for the first time) go way over the word limit. The challenge then is to condense the work down to fit the limit set. Each mini saga is written on a standard story card.

> **Practical tip**
>
> You can make the task easier by specifying mini sagas that must fall between, say, fifty and sixty words. Another tactic is to set 'midi sagas' which are around 100 words long. A greater challenge is to write a drabble, which must be exactly 100 words.

CHAPTER 24

The Detective Game

Activity

The aim of this game is to write out a series of 'clues', which collectively suggest an incident. The clues could be worked around images from the grids. So looking at the romance grid (page 110) clues might include –

- A wine glass lies broken on the floor.
- A plane ticket is on the little table in the hallway by the front door.
- The car parked on the driveway won't start.
- A half empty (or half full) bottle of wine stands open on the worktop in the kitchen.
- A ladder is propped up outside the house by the front bedroom window.

Using all or most of these clues, suggest might have happened. The resulting outline can be used to create a story card or one of its variations, or indeed as the basis of a story used in conjunction with many other activities in this book.

Learning benefits

- Develops inferential thinking (working out a scenario or explanation by putting clues together).
- Shows children a new way of planning stories.
- Gives children control over the amount and complexity of information they can process.

Taking it further

- Although the clues above were based on the Romance Grid, ask children to use them in creating a story in a different genre – a Fantasy, a Murder Mystery, etc.
- Cut out many images and put them in an envelope. Children draw them out at random and make a list of clues that 'takes the mind by surprise' to suggest a story.

- Use the **Coin Flip Plotting Game** (page 79) to ask closed questions about the clues. This will throw up many alternative possibilities for what might have happened.

- Create a grid of clues such as the one in Figure 24.1. Each child in the class could contribute one clue. The grid could be genre specific or generalized. Use as a standard grid (see the section on making and using the 6×6 grids, pages 93–4). Note that the example given here does not feature clues along the bottom row: as children play the game of choosing boxes at random, if they land on a bottom row box they have to invent a clue there and then.

- **Sliding Scale**. Draw a line on the board and mark it 1–5, or ask the class simply to imagine such a scale. Once children are familiar with the idea of putting clues together to suggest stories, begin to locate them along the scale. A highly likely and believable scenario would count as 1, a weird and wonderful tale would be 5. Once you have examples at these two extremes, begin to challenge the group by asking for, say, a three-out-of-five Fantasy story, or a two-out-of-five Wild West tale. The purpose of this activity is to give children more control over their imaginations. You can also apply this 'believability tool' analytically when you study texts with the group. See also *Things Happen for Reasons* at pages 21–3.

The TV is on standby	There is two days' worth of mail in the hallway	An empty milkbottle stands on the kitchen worktop	The number of the house is 42	Ten years ago the garden shed burned down	A cold up of tea is on the side table in the lounge
The Phillips family lives here	The children's school is two miles away	The boxroom upstairs is always kept locked	There is an oil stain on the drive	Three pink rose bushes and a red one grow in the back garden	The DVD machine records the same programme each week
The son is twelve years old	Mrs Phillips collects stamps and old books	There are fresh footprints in the flower border	Mr Phillips had a plumbing business that went bankrupt	A telephone number has been scrawled on the wall by the phone	Flowers in the front room have died
The lock on the garden shed has been forced	A bottle of milk in the kitchen has gone sour	There are five messages on the telephone answering machine	The bed in the main bedroom is unmade	There are a week's worth of newspapers by the bed	The spare house key is missing from the hook in the hallway
A faded red stain can be seen on the stair carpet	Mr Phillips's old school friend called round two days ago	There is money in a tin on the mantel piece in the lounge	The family owns a very valuable pedigree cat	Neighbours say the family keeps itself to itself	A guidebook to New Zealand lies on the coffee table in the front room
Clue 1	Clue 2	Clue 3	Clue 4	Clue 5	Clue 6

Figure 24.1

CHAPTER 25

Settings

In the same way children learn that stories have a beginning, a middle and an end, so they understand that the main components of a story are the plot, characters and setting or background. A creative approach to storymaking helps children to realize that a narrative will grow 'organically': you can start anywhere and eventually it will take shape. Similarly plot, characters and background 'arise together' in the imagination. Thinking about where the story happens will give insights into how the characters behave, which in turn will influence the run of events that form the plot. The setting is not simply the stage on which the characters perform, but the world in which they are embedded.

Activity

Simple settings can be created by choosing images from the grids:

- Place an image on a large sheet of paper for the children to 'draw beyond it'. In the same way that they used their imaginations in the picture masking activity (pages 7–8), so they can visualize where a roadway might go, what could lie at the end of the canyon, where the doorway leads to, etc.

- Stick multiple copies of an image on to a sheet to build a landscape. Photocopying images at different degrees of enlargement creates a sense of perspective – bigger trees in the foreground, smaller versions in the distance. I've found that many children enjoy map making and colouring in as part of the storymaking process.

Practical tip

Map making can be done on the computer and maps are easily created in a Word document. Insert the image and position where needed. Then you can copy-and-paste, resize and position the pictures as you want.

Learning benefits

- Offers a visual field where children can literally place characters and plot ideas.
- Begins to link settings with events.
- Suggests another strategy for planning.
- Incorporates a kinaesthetic element into planning, which some children appreciate.

Taking it further

- Create a landscape as above. If creating on the computer, print out the map and place on the tabletop. Scatter a handful of images relevant to the story across the map. Use where they fall to make creative connections about the plot. So, for instance, if the jeep image lands near the river, the plot idea could be that the driver tried to ford the water but the engine cut out. If the image of money lands nearby, then maybe the driver has been to the mountains to recover hidden loot. This 'scatter gun' technique is another way of using randomness and chance to spark ideas.

- **The Coin Flip Plotting Game**. Create a map, draw in the cardinal compass points and place two or three counters in the middle of the sheet. These represent characters. At this stage it's not necessary to know anything else about the story. Explain to the children that you are looking for two ideas at each step of the game (if more than two are generated these can be kept for later). Begin by saying something like, 'These characters face sudden danger, what could it be?' Use the first two ideas that come along – they are attacked by bandits/one of the characters pulls a gun on his friends. Designate one 'heads', the other 'tails' and flip the coin to see which idea is used.

    Let's suppose the characters are attacked by bandits. Say 'Now what could they do?' – fight or run. Flip the coin. They run. To decide in which direction they run, use a spinner or number the compass points 1–4 and roll a dice. Mark this on the map. 'As they run, they face a different problem. What could it be?' And so on. The value of the game is

    - It accommodates group work and allows everyone to contribute.
    - It takes the pressure off children to 'try and make up a story'.
    - It generates a useful store of plot ideas. The ones that are not used can be noted and used later.
    - It creates a sense of pace and excitement in the plot.
    - It integrates plot, characters and setting 'organically'.

CHAPTER 26

Comic Cuts

Activity

As an aside to the drawing-and-colouring theme, some children enjoy making stories in comicbook format. For those who are not skilled artists (though some kids I've met are brilliant!), the images may be of use. Template pages can be created in Word[1] and panels made using the Rectangle, Line and Autoshapes tools. The WordArt facility offers a huge variety of styles – Booms, Pows, Biffs and Zaps are generated in moments, and individual words or phrases can be moved freely around the page to fit into the panels made earlier. You'll find my modest effort in Figure 26.1.

Practical tip

A quick search on the Internet will help you find further resources. One useful website I came across is http://www.teachchildrenesl.com/filez8932/lesson%20plans/comic_strip.pdf

Learning benefits

- Helps to develop 'visual literacy', specifically the visual conventions of the comicbook.
- Raises awareness of how dialogue supports the telling of a story.
- Gives experience of succinctness in writing.

Figure 26.1

Note

1 This is just one option. You and/or the children may well know other ways of creating comics.

CHAPTER 27

Character Creation

Sometimes the characters in stories written by children are nothing more than names, or may be only minimally described. In helping children to think of characters with some depth, bear the following points in mind:

- Writers should know more about their characters than they put into the story.
- Think about the characters' personalities as well as just physical appearance.
- Make characters consistent. Their behaviour shouldn't change dramatically, unless this happens for good reasons that form a necessary part of the story.
- Characters can develop through the story and learn more about themselves – the hero's journey is a basic example of this.

Activity

Character Creation Game. Cut out images from the grids and put them in an envelope. Make a list of things you want to find out about your character and his/her life. Some ideas are suggested below:

Character profile:

Character's name:
Age: Male / Female: Nationality:
General appearance:

Hair colour, length, style:

Colour of eyes:

Distinguishing features:

General personality type:

Best character trait:

Biggest fault:

Favourite food: TV programme: Hero: Colour:

Likes:

Dislikes:

Habits:

Pets and/or favourite possessions:

Best friend:

Greatest dislike (person or thing):

Best experience so far:

Ambition:

Secret desire:

Children can either simply decide on these, or can pick an image at random from the envelope to offer a clue. It's useful here to bear in mind the idea of 'artful vagueness' (see page 70). The image will tell you *something about* the aspect of the character being investigated. This means that a leap of the imagination will be needed to connect the image with the information you want.

So if for 'biggest fault' you pick the image of a crow, possible answers include:

- My character tends to crow (grumble) about things.
- My character and his/her friends gang up on people.
- My character is a pest.

Sometimes a chain of reasoning will be called for to translate an image into information connected to the characteristic you're exploring. So – secret desire – Joker . . . Joker – cards – gambling – taking risks – not being so cautious in life. Or – favourite possession – image of a spiderweb . . . spiderweb – Indra's Net (a Hindu image of all the stars in the universe being linked by a gleaming net) – jewels – jewellery.

Taking it further

- As children become more experienced at both noticing creative connections as they spring to mind *and* constructing logical chains of reasoning, you can use the images as a way of developing metaphorical thinking. This is simply where an image is taken not to be literally true but figuratively true.
- As an example we can use the image of mountains and say to the class 'This picture tells us something about our character's good (heroic) qualities . . .' Answers I've heard include brave, determined, confident, good at teamwork (since climbing a mountain is a collaborative effort), aims high, wants to get to the top. Notice how this last response can be used in different contexts, most immediately 'wanting to be the best'; i.e. it can easily be used figuratively.
- Making the image more stylized generates even more responses. Figure 27.1. shows how I altered the image of the mountain.

84 ENRICHING THE STORY

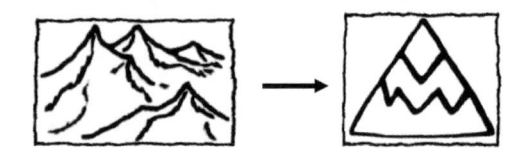

Figure 27.1

Now responses included:

- He likes parties because it looks like a party hat.
- This character is moody because the zigzag line reminds me of 'ups and downs'.
- She's magic because it looks like a wizard's hat.
- This character enjoys the great outdoors. The picture reminds me of a wigwam and I imagine it is in the middle of a grassy plain.
- This person likes history because it reminds me of an Egyptian pyramid.

■ Matching other simple images with ideas such as the following helps children to learn a lot about their characters very quickly: see Figure 27.2.

This tells us something about the character's bad side.

This tells us something about the character's childhood

This tells us something about the character's family

This tells us something about the character's future

This tells us something about the character's attitude

This tells us something about the character's beliefs

Figure 27.2

Learning benefit

This activity in turn allows children to realize the extent to which we use figurative expressions in our language, and to apply that knowledge in their own reading and writing.

SECTION 4
Story Grids

CHAPTER 28

Zig Zag Story Game

Almost all of the images used so far in the book have been taken from the grids featured on pages 102–12. In fact I devised the idea of an image grid for storymaking before most of the other techniques were developed. Creating one 6x6 means that dice rolls can be used to select images at random, as I'll explain shortly. However the simplest way of using the grid is to start in the top left-hand corner and play the Zig Zag Story Game.

Activity

- Explain to the children (whether they work alone or in groups) that they will be rolling the dice a number of times to find out what their story will be about.
- Start in the top left-hand corner. The first roll of the dice will take you along the top row. Wherever you land you'll find out something about how your story starts.
- The next dice roll might take you around on to the second row. Wherever you land you'll discover something about what happens next. Keep rolling the dice and zig zag your way down the board (like snakes and ladders backwards!). By the time you reach the bottom row, the last one or two things the dice chooses for you will tell you something about how the story ends.

Note the use of the artfully vague 'will tell you something about' phrasing. The child has a specific task to carry out, but enough 'creative space' to have ideas of their own. This game offers a simple linear 'and then' sequence that the child can embellish just as they like.

Learning benefit

- Shows children a simple 'linear' way of constructing narrative that will act as a bridge to more sophisticated storymaking using the same resource.

> **Practical tip**
>
> Some children follow the zig zag pattern rigorously, while others start that way but then begin to choose images for themselves anywhere on the grid. This is fine, as long as they can tell you why they've selected particular words and pictures.

Taking it further

You can change images on any grid to suit yourself and/or allow the children to replace some images for themselves. This allows them to use characters, settings, themes, etc., that they're already interested in and blend them into the material you offer.

CHAPTER 29

Grids and Basic Narrative Elements

Activity

- For this activity you must explain to children that they'll use dice rolls to find the 'co-ordinates' of different images. This means the number of the first roll must be counted *underneath the bottom row*. No picture has been selected yet. This is important, because some children count along the row and land on the wrong pictures. Next, roll the dice again and count upwards. Then you will come to the image selected. It's the old technique of 'along the corridor and up the stairs'.

- Having established the procedure, tell the children that they will select an image for each of the basic narrative elements (see page 52). So roll the dice twice and wherever you land the picture will tell you something about the hero in the story. The next double-roll will tell you something about the villain.

- Keep rolling to find out something about the problem, the journey, the partner, etc. . . .

Learning benefits

- Creates a specific and 'concrete' context for becoming familiar with the basic narrative elements.
- Acts as a quick and effective planning tool for storymaking.

Practical tip

Again this is a simple straightforward task that allows a creative space for the children's own ideas. By the time they've gone through those narrative elements many children will have the overview for a story all worked out. Use other story strand techniques to help them build upon this framework.

CHAPTER 30

Following the Question Trail

Activity

The 'full blown' use of the grids proceeds as follows.

- Using double-dice rolls pick two images from a chosen grid. Tell children that as soon as the second image is chosen, it will be put together with the first to create an idea for the story. Saying this 'primes' the children with a positive suggestion that helps them to subconsciously preprocess the material on the grid. In other words they are already making connections before they roll the dice. You may have children who say at this point 'Oh, I've just had an idea. I know what my story will be about!' Acknowledge the idea and allow them to write it down, but insist they roll the dice to get *another* idea too.

- When the idea is clear, ask the child to think of a question about it. What I say is – 'Writers are nosy people, and what I want to know is . . .' Once the question is asked, say, 'Do a double-roll to choose a further image from the grid. That will give you the answer to your question, or at least a clue to the answer.'

- When the question has been answered, draw another question out of what you know. Double-roll to get the answer (or a clue). Then ask a further question about what you've just learned. Double-roll for the answer – and so on, following the question trail.

- Keep going until you either have the story worked out, or enough of the plot to create the rest for yourself.

Learning benefits

- Keeps thinking fresh and flexible. The use of randomness through the use of dice rolls 'takes the mind by surprise' and helps to break the habit of routine thinking.
- Familiarizes children with the motifs (constituent features) and conventions of the chosen genre.
- Gives teachers and/or children control over the subject matter of the story.
- Supports group discussion and collaborative storymaking.
- Makes storymaking a more memorable experience and aids subsequent recall of the narratives.

Practical tip

Sometimes children start to become overwhelmed by the amount of information they generate. Or they may get lost or stuck and not know what to think next. If this happens I tell them to 'leap to the end of the story. Do a double-roll and wherever you land on the grid, that picture will tell you something about how the story ends.'

This means they've got the early part of the narrative organized, an unknown middle section and an idea for the ending. This usually allows them to connect the beginning with the end: either the middle part of the story becomes clear or as they continue to double-roll for more images, these slot into place and allow the middle to make sense.

Worked example

Using the Wild West grid on page 112:

- Gallows (3/4) and 'Ride' (1/5). My idea is that two cowboys are riding quickly to escape being hanged for a crime they didn't commit – I've decided these characters will be the hero and his partner.
- Question: What crime are they accused of? Stagecoach (1/4) – holding up a stagecoach.
- What was so valuable on the stagecoach? Gates (3/6) – I'm using this to mean an opportunity (a gateway) to go on an adventure.
- What kind of adventure? Wagons (4/2) – a chance to make a new life in a different part of the country.
- But I still don't see why that should make someone hijack the stagecoach . . . Canyon (2/5). I don't have an idea about this so I'll come back to it later.
- I want to know something about the villain in the story. Rope (2/1) or it could be a snake. My villain is a 'snake', very sly and dangerous. He's also a wealthy cattle rancher (rope – lasso – cattle).
- How can I connect him to the chance to be a pioneer in another part of the country? Coin (5/6) – he can make a lot of money from either building more ranches there or staking a claim to the land and selling it off.
- Eureka! I think the canyon could be a danger point on the journey to the new country. Maybe the villain could set an ambush there.
- How are the hero and villain connected? Telegraph wires (2/2). They've never met but only sent each other telegrams. Eureka! That's why the villain feels safe – the hero's never seen him. That would make it easier to frame the hero.
- Leap to the end of the story. Barrels (4/3) – I'm thinking barrels of oil. The villain somehow knows that the new country is rich in oil. Eureka! Someone on the stagecoach had proof of that and the villain wanted to steal it (and maybe kill the passengers too). That way, no one would suspect the villain's real motives for being part of the pioneering wagon train. So the end of the story will be about how his evil plan is discovered and how the new settlers can drill for oil for themselves. They name their new land Texas.

👍 Learning benefits

- Encourages active questioning.
- Illustrates the idea that there is always a solution if a child gets stuck in making up a story.
- Reinforces the logical consistency of the narrative and the idea that events happen for reasons that make sense within the context of the story.

💡 Practical tips

I hope this gives you a flavour of how the game can work. You can 'scaffold' the activity to suit the age/ability levels of the group: by working through the plot with them, making the grid smaller, changing some of the images to make them less ambiguous, etc. However I've found that children as young as Year 4 can cope with the 6×6 grids, especially if you guide (not spoon-feed) them towards making connections.

➡ Taking it further

Focus the follow-the-question-trail idea into a game of reasoning. Use 'because' to invite sound reasons for what happens in the story. The hero and his partner were on the run because – they were going to be hanged. They were going to be hanged because – they'd been accused of holding up a stagecoach. The accusation was false because – the villain tried to frame them . . . and so on. Such a game of because can happen as children create the narrative, or as a review technique once the planning has been done. In any case it serves to check the logical consistency of the story to make sure it 'works'.

CHAPTER 31

Making Grids

Activity

You'll appreciate that 6x6 grids are easily created, and once made serve as a permanent resource. In creating my selection I bore the following points in mind:

- Use a mixture of words and pictures.
- Words that can have several meanings are better.
- Some images must be 'genre specific' (so that children can keep within the genre as they learn more about its conventions).
- Other images can be general objects, aspects of the landscape, etc.
- Some ambiguous images give scope for speculation and varied use.

Learning benefits

One benefit of making your own grids is that you have control over their content and therefore what the children will think about. The grids offer flexibility within a structure. The images you offer and the techniques for accessing them provide children with specific tasks and systematic methods for carrying them out. At the same time, the context of any grid invites creative connections (i.e. new ideas) to be made. This gives children a sense of ownership of their work, even though you have dictated the components they use to construct their stories.

Taking it further

- To add variety to the children's stories, change some of the images in the grids from time to time.
- Delete some of the pictures and invite children to replace them with others of their own.
- Encourage children to make grids based on favourite stories. Grids made from pictures cut out of comics are highly colourful and work very well.

- Tell the class a fairy tale and ask groups to create a grid based on the story. You'll find that each group will make a slightly (and sometimes not so slightly) different grid.
- Help children to create grids on the computer. My method initially was to open a Word file, create a 6x6 table and import pieces of clip art into the cells (from a clip art CD, although lots of images can be found online). Extend children's skills by asking them to edit pictures in a graphics application: images can be resized, the colours changed, greyscaled, cropped, etc.

Taking it even further

- Images can be inserted into Word documents, so if stories are written on PCs pictures can be dropped into the text to add visual appeal, and arranged so that the words wrap around the picture.
- Go 3D. Use a 6x6 checkerboard and place real objects in the squares. Children can handle the objects selected by dice rolls to bring a tactile dimension to their storymaking.

CHAPTER 32

Grids and Topic Areas

Activity

Although the grids were originally designed for storymaking, they can also be used in a non-fictional context. The most immediate way of doing this is to help children to use and become familiar with the 'vocabulary of the subject'. I realized the value of this when a school asked me to link the creative writing workshops I was going to do with some classes to a topic the year group had started on the Anglo-Saxons. The best way I could think of for doing this was to have an Anglo-Saxon grid made up specially. I asked the class teachers what words and pictures they would prefer, then I commissioned an artist to draw it up for me (which is why the style is different from the other grids – see page 103).

Learning benefit

As children created stories using the grid – although they were not necessarily historically accurate – they were making connections between ideas relevant to the topic and becoming more familiar with the terms they would use in writing non-fictional pieces about Anglo-Saxons. And as Rudyard Kipling said, 'If history were taught in the form of stories, it would never be forgotten.'

Taking it further

That basic activity can be enhanced by placing topic-specific terms around the grid and asking children to build them into their stories where they can. See Figure 32.1.

A variation of this technique makes use of the narrative line: arrange images and keywords along the line that tell the story of the historical episode being studied. A little imagination will reveal further applications of the idea – in one school we created an African adventure grid so that children could make stories about conservation, including the conflict between trying to save rare species and local people wanting to extend grazing land for their animals. One group wrote a parallel story

96 STORY GRIDS

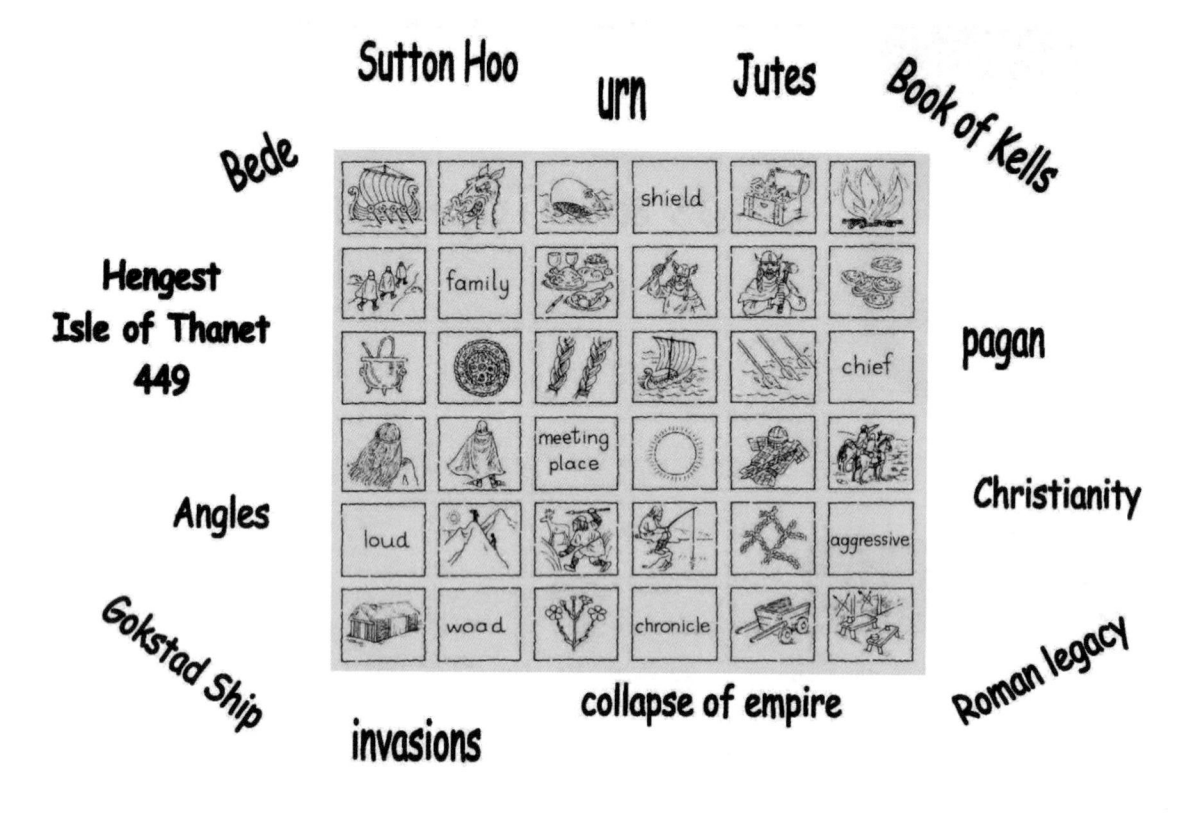

Figure 32.1

(see pages 63–4) from the villagers' viewpoint, since earlier the farmers had been portrayed as villains. The class discussion that followed took the form of a simple dialectic – a reasoned discussion where different viewpoints were expressed within a shared context, out of which ideally arise some points of agreement and directions towards a solution.

> **Practical tip**
>
> One important point I want to make about using image grids in a non-fictional way is that even if the stories are about aliens or rampaging Egyptian mummies or animals that talk (i.e. pure fiction), the activity is helping to *steep the child in the subject*. I became interested in Science Fiction (SF) from an early age and that in turn led to a fascination for astronomy, and from there to other sciences. I tell children that it was *because* I loved SF that I became fascinated by and coped with science in school. Other areas of interest in my life – mythology, psychology, linguistics – arose because I was captivated by Fantasy and Horror stories in childhood. And as every good teacher knows, what fires a child's imagination can lead to a lifelong passion. In that regard, and perhaps the final validation of taking time and effort to help children create stories, is Emerson's conviction that 'Imagination is not a talent of some men, but is the health of every one.'

CHAPTER 33

Story Strings

Earlier I suggested that you could bring a tactile dimension to children's storymaking by using real objects on a tabletop instead of flat images on paper. Out of that idea developed the technique I call story strings. These are selections of interesting beads knotted on a string. The string represents the narrative line and the beads can be characters, objects, events and other motifs[1] a child can use in a story. (See Figure 33.1).

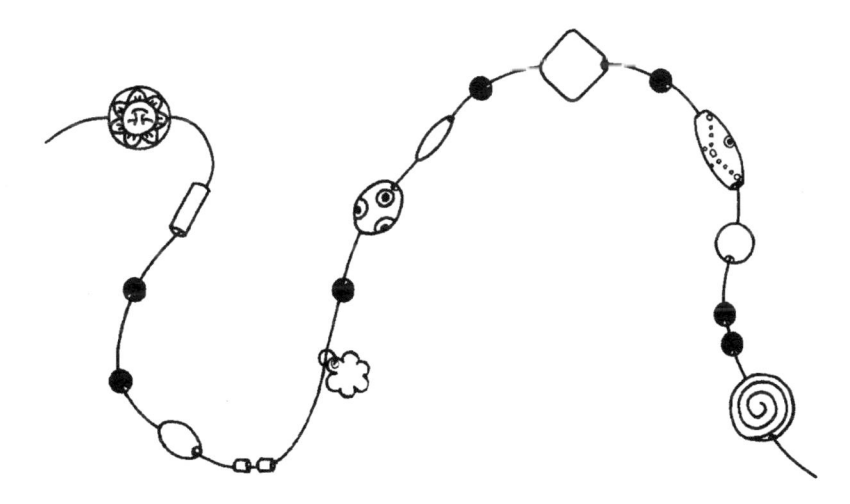

Figure 33.1

> ## Practical tips
>
> Story strings work best, I've found, working one-to-one with a child. It's helpful if the child has already done some work on metaphorical thinking (see page 83–4). This opens up many more possibilities as to what a bead could be. For instance in the example shown in Figure 33.1, looking at the two black beads close together, 10-year-old Ben decided at first that they were two people floating in the sea. Then he had a Eureka moment and said, 'But they also stand for two nights. Those people have been trying to survive in the sea for all of that time!' You'll find further examples of how young writers worked with story strings on the website.

You can do some preparatory work with the whole class by showing them pictures of individual beads and following the pattern of 'if this told us something about . . .' we looked at on page 87. Once children are familiar with interpreting abstract-looking beads in the context of a character or setting, etc., show them two beads and say, 'If this told us something about the relationship between the hero and his partner, what do we learn?' Gradually you can build up to longer sequences of beads, so that it's then an easy leap into the full-blown use of story strings.

Searching for suitable beads takes some time (you'll find bead shops in many cities and there are also online dealers), but once you have them making the story strings is easy. There's no need to have any story in mind as you thread the beads: in fact this can work against you as you may be tempted to influence a child's ideas if you've already decided what the story should be about. Strings may be made of varying lengths with different numbers of beads, which can be more or less 'abstract' and representational. In working with younger children it's obviously better to have a short string of beads depicting real objects such as flowers, bees, shoes, etc. (again see the examples on the website).[2]

Activity

- Whatever the age of the child or the degree of complexity of the story string, let the child take it in their hands and explain that the beads tell a story, although we don't know what it is yet. Ask the child first to decide which end of the string is the start of the story.

- Look at the first bead and say, 'So if this told us something about how the story starts, what do we learn?' Obviously you will use your professional judgement in deciding how far to guide and prompt the child, but don't spoon feed ideas.

- Allow the child to 'handle his/her way' along the string. Suggest as necessary that every good story needs a villain, a problem, etc. Reminding about basic narrative elements is fine.

- If a child starts to flounder or get stuck, use the 'leap to the end' trick to get things untangled. Say, 'Let's look at the last bead. If this told us something about how the story ends, what do we learn?' This often gets the ball (or the bead) rolling again.

- Be aware that it isn't necessary to use every bead. If a child can't make sense of particular beads and build them into the story, just move on. It may well be that the bead will spark an idea later. If you find that some children really do struggle to use a story string, try combining them with a standard grid. Delete some images on a grid, lay it flat on the table and place a bead or two in each of the empty boxes. Use dice rolls to choose images and beads at random, as explained earlier.

Learning benefits

- Story strings are a permanent, relatively cheap but very flexible resource. It's likely that every child will come up with a different story from any given string.

- Working with the string focuses attention and develops concentration. So-called kinesthetic learners especially can benefit from the physical manipulation of the bead strings.
- Using more abstract beads develops children's powers of speculation and interpretation.
- Using several identical strings with a group stimulates discussion, problem solving, decision making and collaborative creation.
- Once a story has been created using a bead string, handling the same string subsequently aids children's memory of the tale. The word 'remember' literally means 'to bring back into the members' – to recreate the body memory, the feelings and physical sensations evoked originally.
- Story strings can be turned into wonderful fashion accessories!

Taking it further

- Instead of beads on a string suggesting a narrative, let them represent a character. Go through the character traits checklist on pages 82–3 and use the beads to say 'something about' personality type, likes/dislike, favourite food, etc.
- Use beads with settings maps (page 78). Having established the basic landscape – city streets, forests and mountains, desert with dunes and canyons, etc. – scatter some beads across the map and let them represent incidents and events, story ingredients (page 47), topics for dialogue – in fact anything that will enrich the basic plot.

Notes

1 By this I mean a constituent feature that helps to define and describe the context of the story. Snippets of dialogue, small descriptive details – virtually anything can be used as a motif to 'tag' a story as SF, Horror, Romance, etc.
2 If you would like to try story strings but have difficulty finding suitable beads or the time to create the strings, we can make them for you to your requirements. For further details email steve@sbowkett.freeserve.co.uk

The value and benefits of making stories are numerous and profound. Being able to generate and organize ideas amounts to a basic and powerful skill that can be used in all areas of learning and life. The Vietnamese poet and monk Thich Nhat Hanh said that life is the instrument by which we search for the truth. Creating stories helps to sharpen that instrument.

Happy storymaking.

Appendix
The Grids

1 Adventure
2 Anglo-Saxon
3 Animal Adventure
4 Egyptian
5 Fantasy
6 Horror
7 Mystery Thriller
8 Pirate
9 Romance
10 Science Fiction
11 Wild West

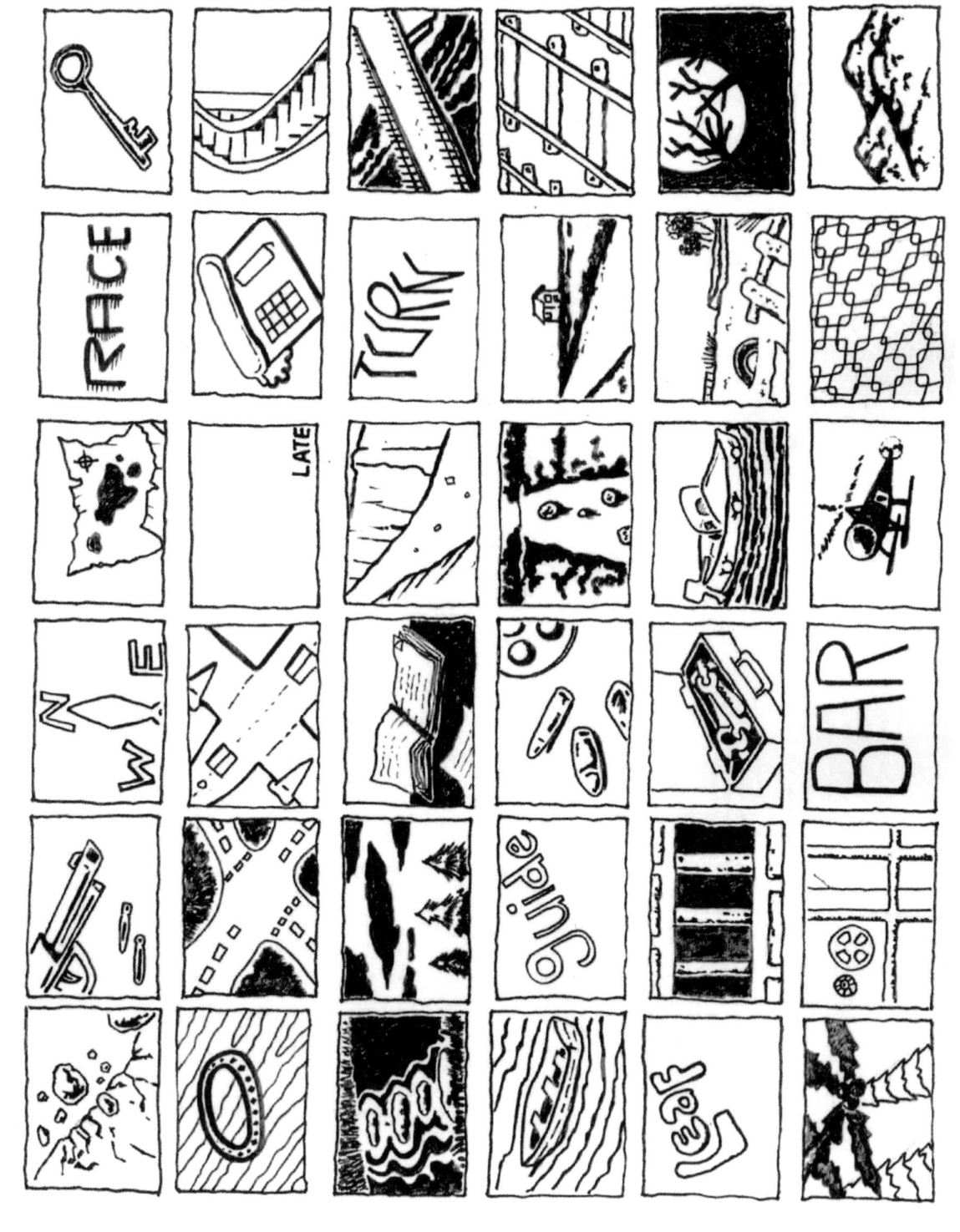

Grid 1: Adventure

Grid 2: Anglo-Saxon

		chief		aggressive	
shield					chronicle
			meeting place		
	family				woad
				loud	

Grid 3: Animal Adventure

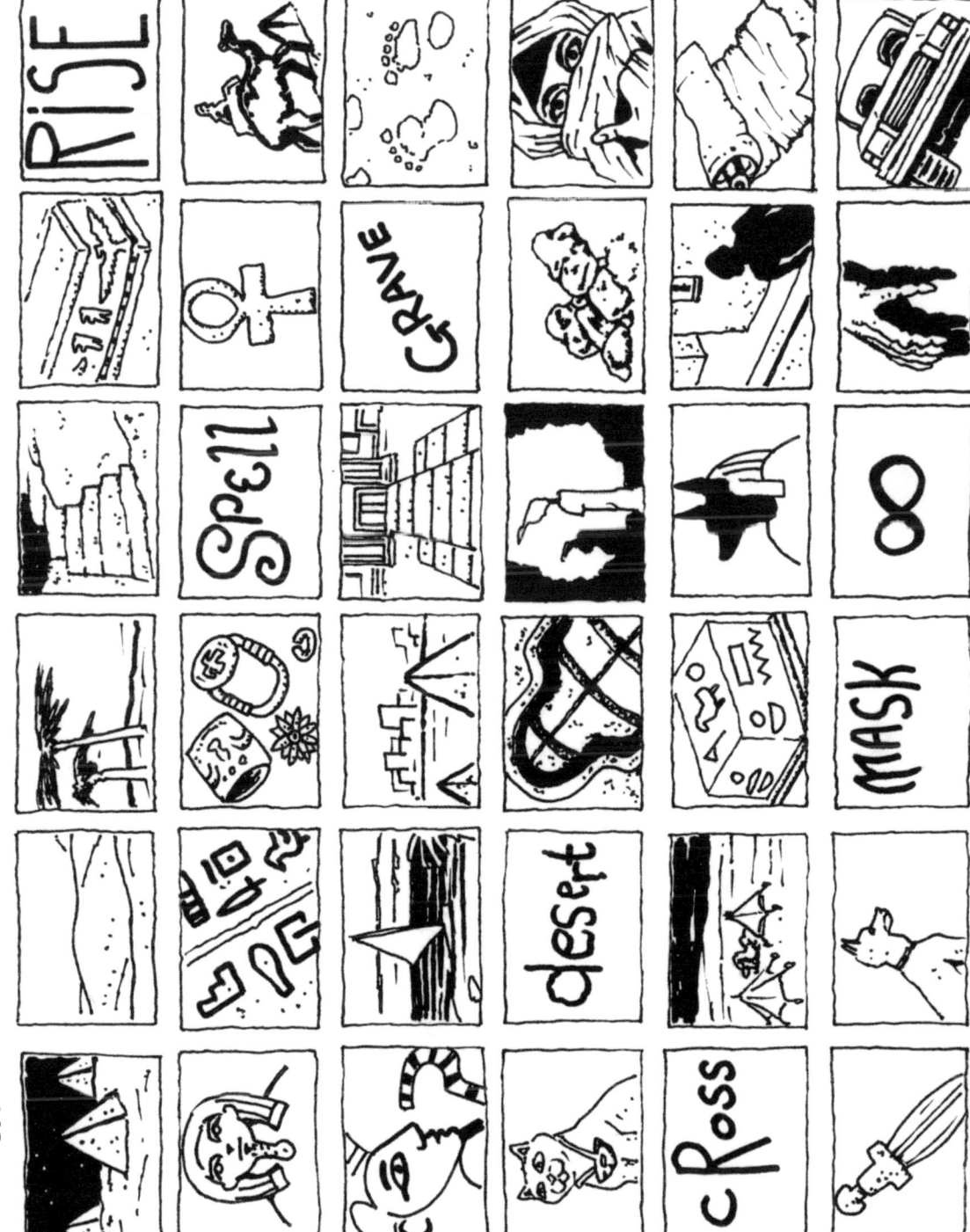

Grid 4: Egyptian

Grid 5: Fantasy

(crack)	(creature)	(hexagon)	lost	(reeds)	(creature)
(arrow)	(boar)	(shooting star)	(masks)	(harp)	(trees)
(roots)	treasure	(shackles)	threshold	(lantern)	guardian
(axe)	(leaves)	(jar)	(triangle)	(plant)	(spider eyes)
(shield)	Boreas	(pattern)	set	(foot)	cross
(castle)	8	(cat)	(hand)	Helcyrian	(lightning)

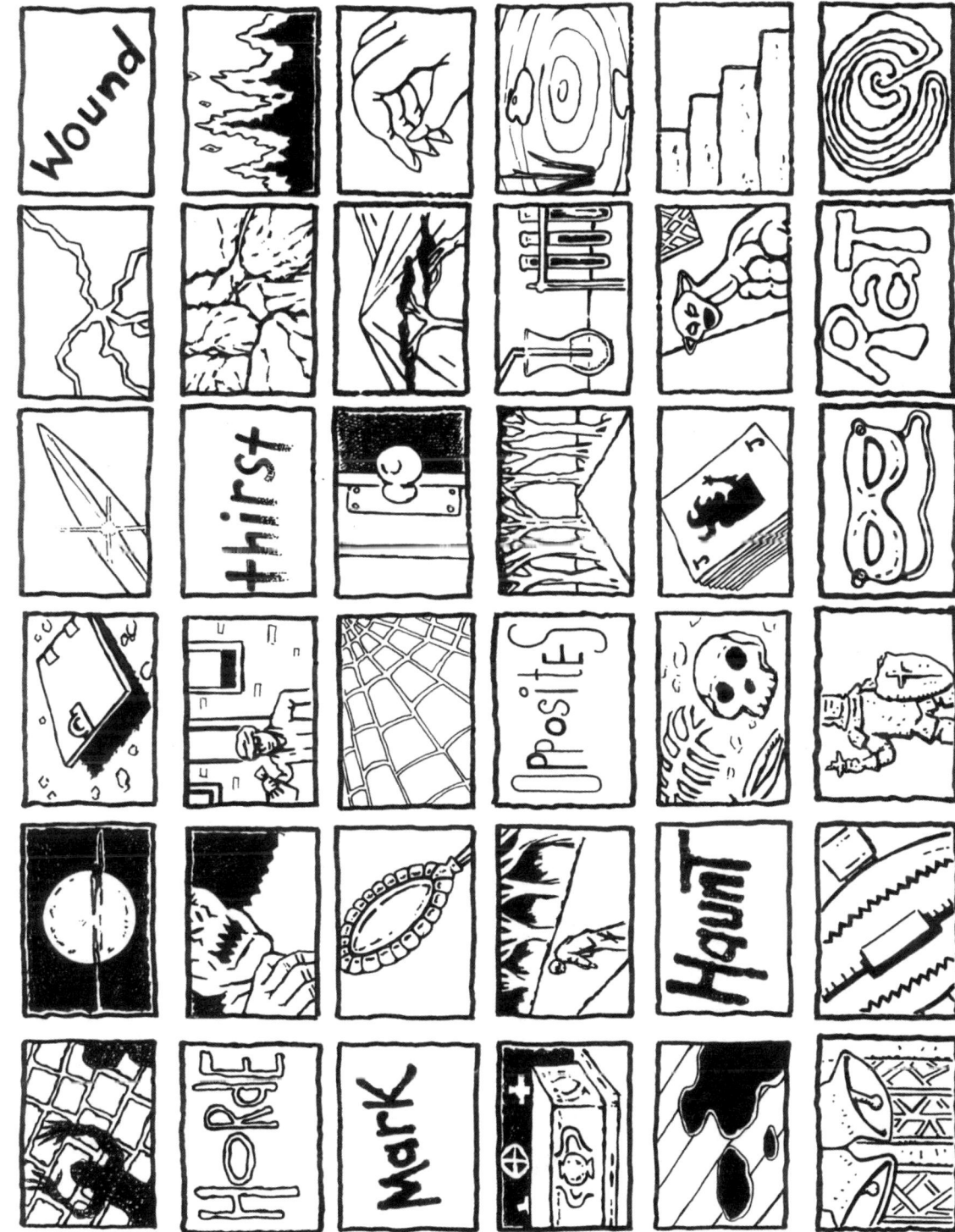

Grid 6: Horror

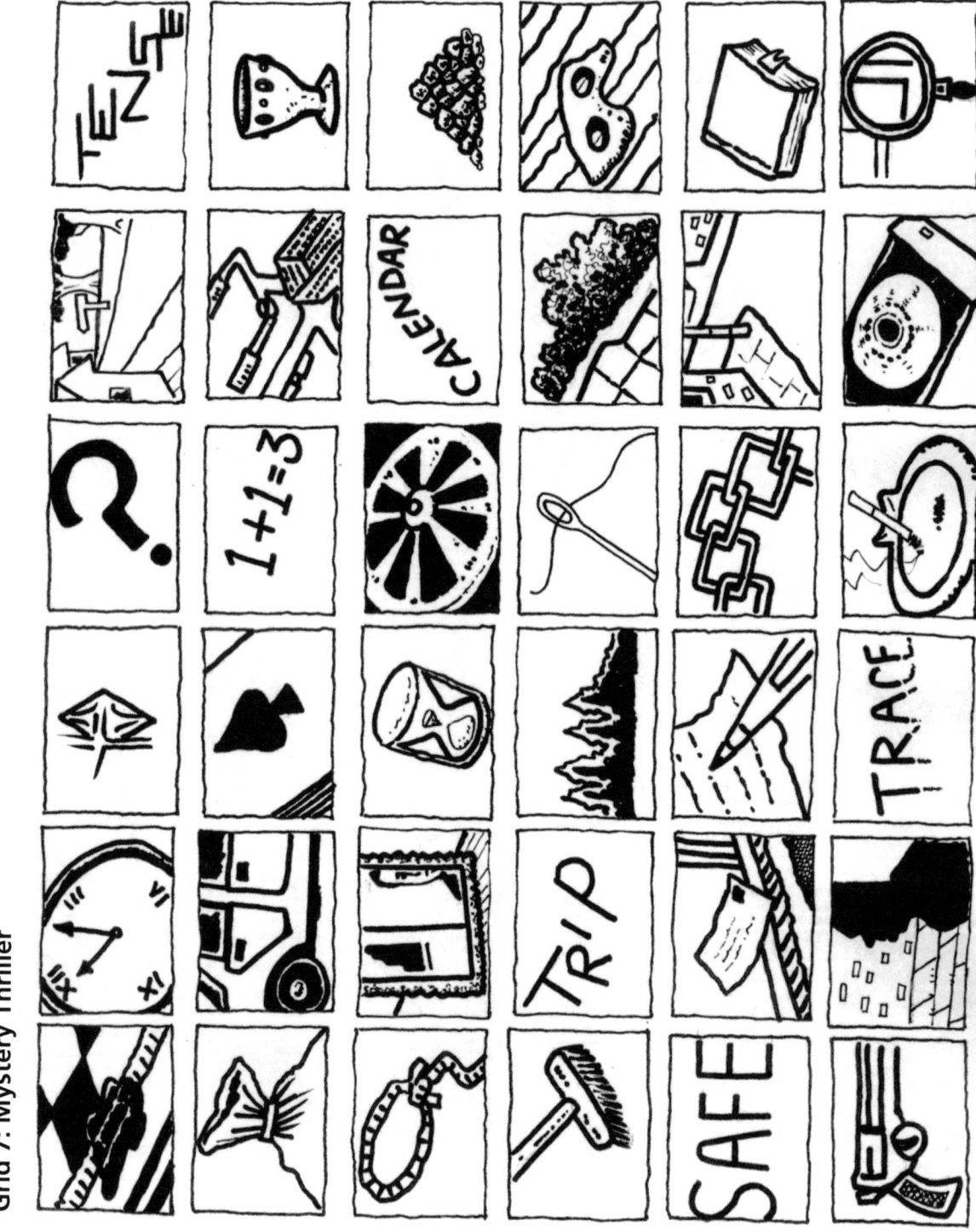

Grid 7: Mystery Thriller

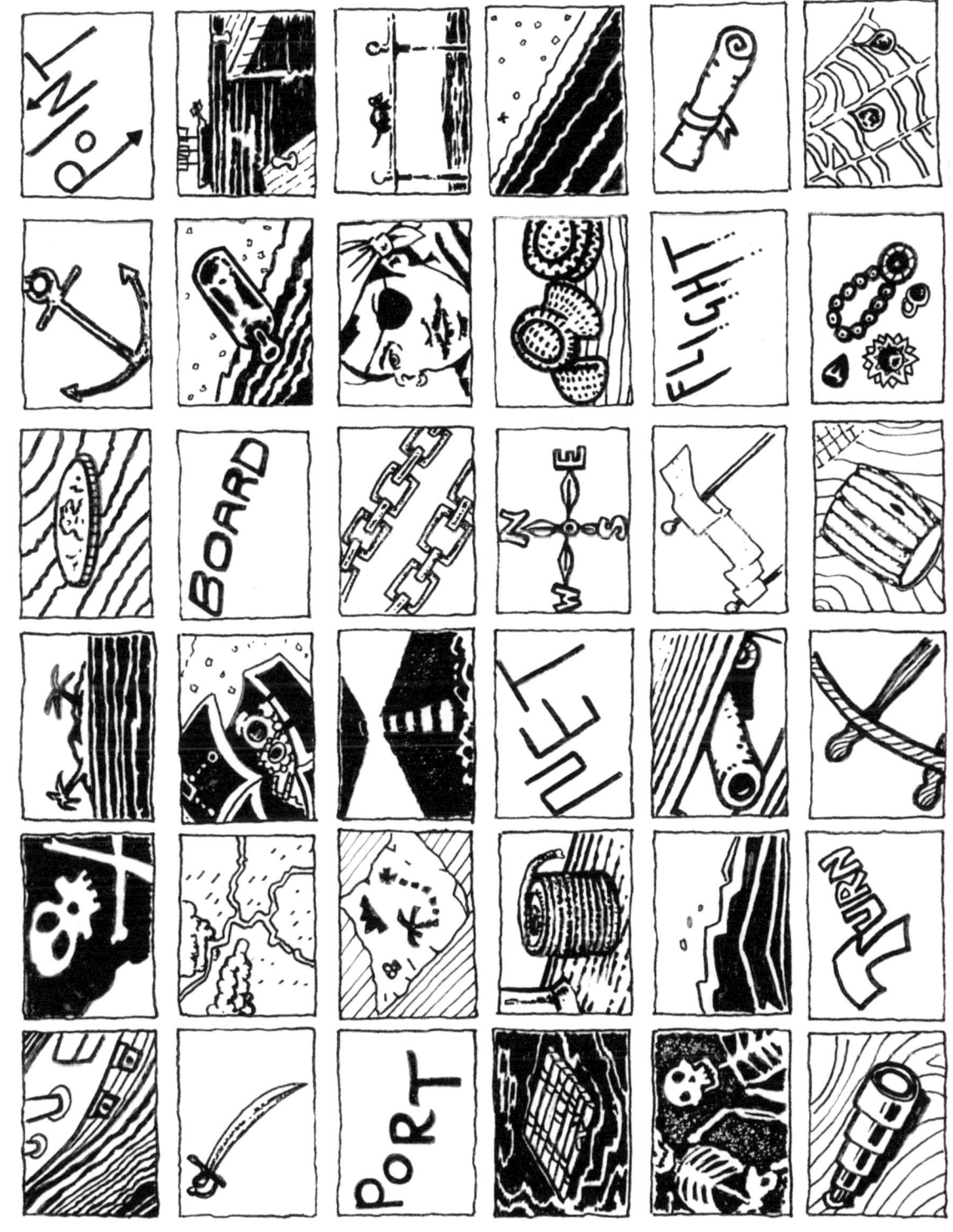

Grid 8: Pirate

Grid 9: Romance

Grid 10: Science Fiction

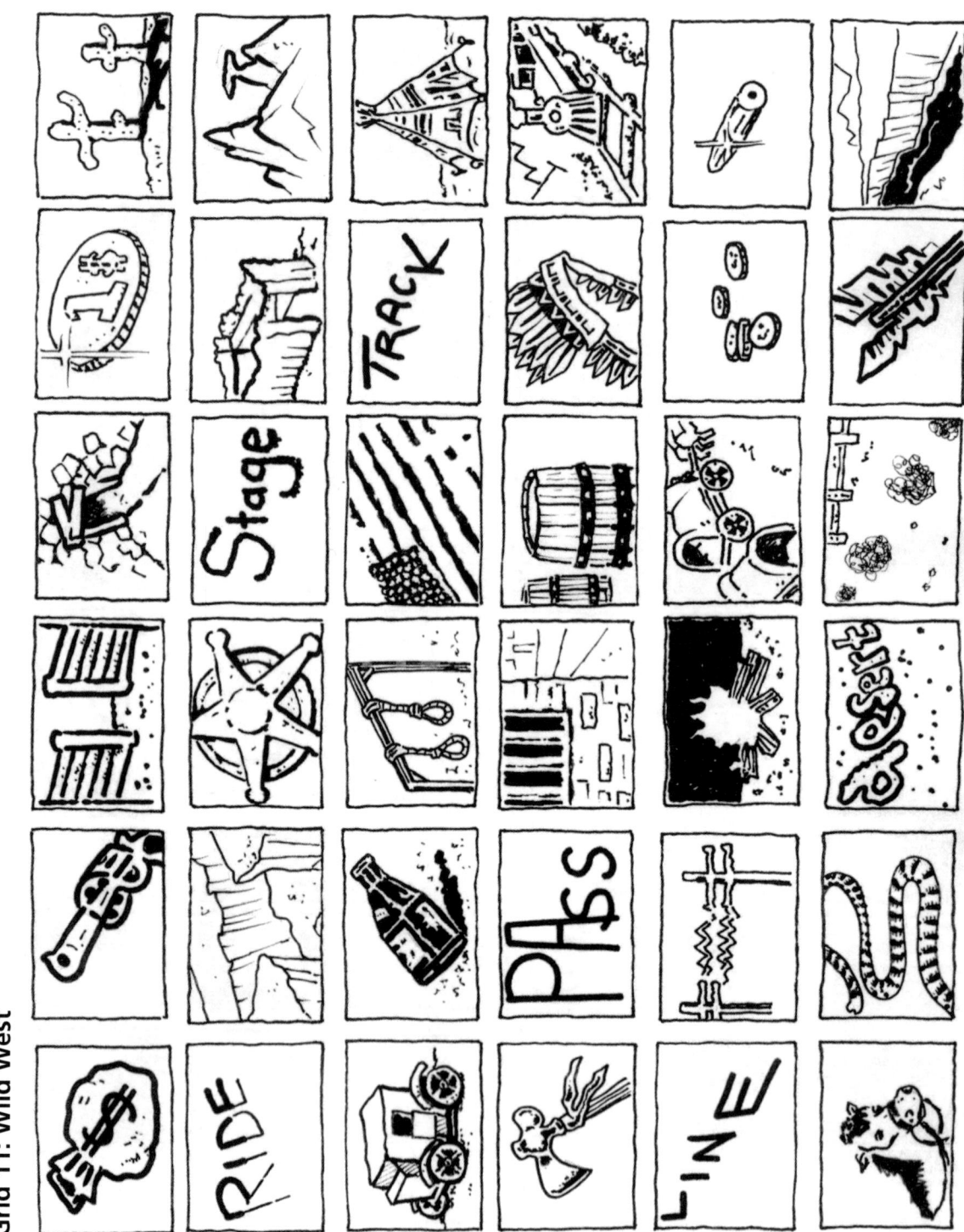

Grid 11: Wild West

Bibliography

Booker, C. (2007) *The Seven Basic Plots*. London: Continuum.

Bowkett, S. (2001) *ALPS StoryMaker: Using Fiction as a Resource for Accelerated Learning*. Stafford: Network Educational Press.

Bowkett, S. (2004) *StoryMaker Catch Pack: Using Genre Fiction as a Resource for Accelerated Learning*. Stafford: Network Educational Press.

Bowkett, S. and Stanley, S. (2004) *But Why? Developing Philosophical Thinking in the Classroom*. Stafford: Network Educational Press.

Bowkett, S. (2008) *Countdown to Creative Writing*. Oxford: Routledge.

Bowkett, S. (2009) *Countdown to Non-Fiction Writing*. Oxford: Routledge.

Jackson, S. and Livingstone, I. (2002) *The Warlock of Firetop Mountain*. Cambridge: Icon Books.

Propp, V. (2001) *Morphology of the Folktale*. Austin, TX: University of Texas Press.

Voytilla, S. (1999) *Myth and the Movies*. Studio City, CA: Michael Wiese Productions.

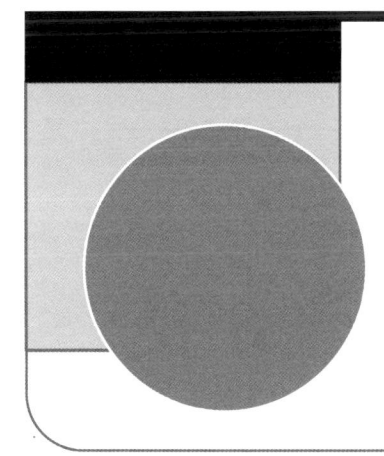

Index

adjectives, selecting to make subtle distinctions 20, 30
'and then' as a bad writing habit 11
'artful vagueness' in prompting ideas 70, 87, 98
associating 9
   see also originality

back story 44
because game, the 23
beginning-middle-end structure of a story 15, 44, 52
brainstorming 9

characters 82, 99
cliffhangers 48
coin-flip technique 69, 79
comics 80
connectives 15, 38
criteria of quality in writing 21

dialogue 18

flashbacks 44

genre
   conventions of 1
   vocabulary of 10, 12

if-then games 8, 69
'ingredients' to affect a story's emotional tone 47
interpreting 12

literacy 2
logical consistency 15, 21
   see also reasonableness

many-endings game 35
'maybe hand', the 8, 21
metacognition 25–6, 29
metaphorical thinking 42, 83, 97
   see also story 'ingredients'
mind mapping 7
motifs 99
multi-sensory thinking 29, 73

narrative 14
   basic elements of 52
   template for 56
noun-to-adjective game 31

originality 1
overview of a story 11, 39, 46
'overwhelm' 2

parts of speech 17, 43, 48
potential, principle of 11, 36
predicting 35

questioning 7, 22, 24, 74, 90

randomness as a spur to creativity 37, 68, 76, 87
reasonableness 77
reasons (behind the events in stories) 8, 21, 53, 92
resolution as a component of narrative structure 56–7

second person in writing 73
seed thoughts 11
sentences, complex 17
sequels 46, 68
settings 78, 99
speculation 7
'stream of consciousness' writing 36
summarizing 11
synonyms 10, 20

third person in writing 39, 73

unmasking picture technique 8

vocabulary, and factual subjects 12, 95

while-game 39
'word morphs' – turning words into different parts of speech 48
word webs see associating

Yin-Yang symbol 53

Related Books from Open University Press
Purchase from www.openup.co.uk or order through your local bookseller

---

CRITICAL THINKING ACROSS THE CURRICULUM
DEVELOPING CRITICAL THINKING SKILLS, LITERACY AND PHILOSOPHY IN THE PRIMARY CLASSROOM

Mal Leicester and Denise Taylor

Learning how to be critical and think for one's self are key development steps in the education process. Developing critical thinking is vital for supporting children to become independent learners.

This fun, practical book is very easy to use in the classroom and is designed to help children:

- Understand key critical thinking concepts.
- Develop critical thinking skills.
- Understand different types of reasoning and knowledge in all areas of the curriculum.
- Draw on their natural wonder and curiosity to engage in philosophical discussion.
- Develop reasoning skills in relation to moral dilemmas and the choices of every day life.

The authors present original beautifully illustrated children's stories that take abstract ideas, philosophical questions and critical skills as their central themes. They make the unfamiliar and complex ideas concrete and easily understandable.

Drawing on the stories and additional photocopiable resources, each chapter then offers a wealth of learning activities. These are designed to help you develop children's critical thinking and practice relevant tools such as asking good questions, giving good reasons or categorising material.

The activities and resources include both subject specific and cross-curricular links and are differentiated for Key Stage 1 and 2. There are also extension activities for enthusiastic, gifted and talented children.

Contents

Introduction - Asking Questions - Point of View - Being Rational -Tools of Critical Thinking: Finding Out - Tools of Critical Thinking: Analysis - An Introduction to Philosophy - Ethics and Morality - Knowledge and Truth - Knowledge as Worthwhile Learning - Problems of Perception - Resources

October 2010   192pp   978-0-335- 23879-8 (Paperback)

BEGINNING TEACHING: BEGINNING LEARNING 3/E
IN PRIMARY EDUCATION

Janet Moyles (ed)

"This collection provides an excellent introduction to the practical skills which all student teachers have to develop but it also celebrates the unpredictability and excitement of working with interested, inquisitive children. [It] should inspire readers to see teaching, in universities as well as in classrooms, as the promotion of lively conversations between learners."

Rod Parker-Rees, University of Plymouth

"The second edition was invaluable and this is even better."

Yvonne Yule, University of Aberdeen

The third edition of this highly successful text sets out to explore some of the wider issues to be investigated by beginning teachers - and those who support them - when working with early years and primary age children, while at the same time, exploring some of the delight and enjoyment in the teaching role.

The book is organised into four parts - Early Beginnings; Beginning to Understand Children's Thinking and Learning; Organising for Teaching and Learning; Supporting and Enhancing Learning and Teaching - and reflects the current context of education and care by covering children from birth to 11-years. There are new chapters covering teaching assistants and interagency working, as well as children's independence and physical activity. Cameos and examples of practice in settings and classrooms help to illustrate the many different aspects of teaching.

Comprehensively revised and updated throughout, this book is written in a lively style and offers guidance, encouragement and support for all those new to working in schools and other educational settings, and gives them the confidence to reflect upon, challenge and enhance their own learning and practices.

Beginning Teaching Beginning Learning is essential reading for all students and newly qualified primary teachers.

Contents
List of Figures and Tables - Notes on the editor and contributors - Acknowledgements - Abbreviations - Introduction - Part 1 Early beginnings - Part 2 Beginning to understand children's thinking and learning - Part 3 Organizing for teaching and learning - Part 4 Supporting and enhancing learning and teaching - Conclusion - Index.

2007   352pp   978-0-335-22130-1 (Paperback)   978-0-335-22131-8 (Hardback)

MIND EXPANDING

TEACHING FOR THINKING AND CREATIVITY IN PRIMARY EDUCATION

Rupert Wegerif

There is growing interest in developing flexible thinking and learning skills in the primary classroom but there has been little agreement as to exactly what these skills are and how best to teach for them.

This innovative book responds to that challenge with a coherent account of what thinking and creativity are and how they can be taught. Taking a 'dialogic' approach, it shows how engaging children in real dialogue is possible in every area of the curriculum and how this can lead to more reflective, considerate and creative children who are able to think for themselves and to learn creatively.

Wegerif explores the success of approaches such as Philosophy for Children, Thinking Together, Dialogic Teaching and Building Learning Power. Using illustrations and activities, he explains how teaching and learning across the primary curriculum can be transformed.

This book is important reading for all primary teachers and trainees who are looking for practical ideas for teaching thinking skills in the primary classroom.

Rupert Wegerif is Professor of Education at the University of Exeter, UK.

Contents
Introduction: Is it really possible to teach thinking? - What is dialogic education? - Creative talk - Creativity explained – Reason - Thinking strategies - ICT and knowledge age skills - Conclusion: Mind Expanding

September 2010   193pp
978-0-335-23373-1 (Paperback)   978-0-335-23374-8 (Hardback)

The McGraw·Hill Companies

Kingscourt Writing Adventures

NEW!

Achieve excellent standards in writing & thinking skills

Kingscourt Writing Adventures are ideal for:

- ✓ Writing
- ✓ Speaking
- ✓ Thinking
- ✓ Listening
- ✓ Creativity
- ✓ Imagination

Created to fit the Primary Framework

Everything you need in one box for each year

'I thoroughly recommend the use of this unique product to any teacher wanting to give their pupils the greatest head start in life – the ability to think creatively and logically to enhance future success and explore all of life's wondrous opportunities.'

Edward De Bono

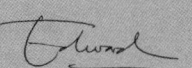

Edward de Bono's Six Thinking Hats

The Blue Hat
The blue hat is used toy study the thinking process.

The Green Hat
The green hat is used for creative thinking and idea generation.

The Red Hat
The red hat is used to express feelings without a need for justification.

The Yellow Hat
The yellow hat is used to outline the good points of an idea with logical supporting reasons.

The Black Hat
The black hat is used for assessing problems.

The White Hat
The white hat is used to gather facts and information.

T: 01628 502 730 • e: kingscourt@mcgraw-hill.com
w: www.kingscourt.co.uk